AWARDS
won by The Farmer's Daughter Restaurant

1. **WINNER OF 5 INTERNATIONAL AWARDS**
   Frankfort, Germany 1968

2. **WINNER OF 2 GOLD MEDALS**
   National Restaurant Association 1968

3. **AWARD: 2 SILVER TROPHIES**
   National Chefs' Association 1968

4. **AWARD: 2 FIRST PRIZE BLUE RIBBONS**
   National Chefs' Association 1968

5. **RESTAURANT OF THE YEAR AWARD**
   Esquire Magazine 1969

6. **FORD MOTOR COMPANY AWARD**
   Restaurant of the Month—July 1969

7. **TOP OF THE TABLE AWARD**
   Hospitality Magazine 1969

8. **MERIT AWARD—TOP 20 IN THE COUNTRY**
   Hospitality Magazine 1970

9. **AWARD: RESTAURANT OF THE MONTH**
   House and Garden Magazine—August 1970

THE
FARMER'S DAUGHTER COOKBOOK

by Kandy Norton Henely

A FAWCETT GOLD MEDAL BOOK

Fawcett Publications, Inc., Greenwich, Conn.

THE FARMER'S DAUGHTER COOKBOOK

Printed in Canada

August 1971

To Mom

Your berry-patch girl looks back on the sunlit days of a perfect childhood—meadows, the brook, the scaled-to-size playhouse. But best of all were the days in your country kitchen—measuring, and rolling, and opening the big black oven door to discovery. This was the joy; this was the contentment; this was the birth of the dream which came to fulfillment and made a success of the Farmer's Daughter Restaurant.

CONTENTS

The Farmer's Daughter Story   1

Stocks   4

Soups and Chowders   7

Vegetables   25

Meats   36

Dressings, Gravies, and Sauces   54

Poultry and Eggs   72

Stuffing   79

Seafood   86

Sandwiches and Snacks   91

Pickling and Canning   97

Salads   147

Salad Dressings   160

Breads and Rolls   168

   Quick Breads   169

   Yeast Breads   187

Cookies   207

Cakes   231

Frostings   255

Pies   271

Desserts   288

Dessert Sauces   299

Miscellaneous   304

INDEX   319

THE
FARMER'S DAUGHTER
COOKBOOK

The Farmer's Daughter Story

I grew up in a berry patch, Mother often told me, and I almost came to believe it. The wide fields below our farm were dotted with wild berries during strawberry season.

When I was too young to walk, Mother would put me under an umbrella on a blanket to keep me from the hot sun. As I grew older, it was my doll that found shelter there while I wandered through the berries after butterflies. When I became tired, I would crawl under the shade and fall asleep with my doll wrapped in my arms. Here Mother would find us, both faces smeared with berries.

Mother would seek the most delectable patches and then call to my brothers and sisters to fill their pails. Only she took the job seriously, but every berry counted. When we saw the farm teams coming homeward, we knew our day in the field was ended.

Each year we looked for the spread of deep red that topped our meadows, so we would be the first ones in the strawberry patches. But this wasn't necessary; we knew a more interesting sign to watch. A neighbor with eleven children lived behind us on the farthest side of Turkeyfoot Hill, and often Mother, a nurse, was called upon to help in an emergency. One winter morning after she had delivered one of the many babies, she asked, "Where are the clean clothes?" Katie looked up surprised and answered, "Ain't got any. I jest wash once a year, in strawberry time." None of us ever forgot this, and when the smell of berries was in the air we would wait until we saw a string of clothes dancing on a sagging line. It was then we knew it was really "strawberry time."

Almost each night, after supper Mother and I took a lighted candle and passed it over the cans of fruit and vegetables that stood in perfect formation against a background of whitewash. The cellar was damp, for a tiny stream coursed across the hard dirt bottom, to disappear under the foundation that walled our basement. As summer passed, it became a fortress of plenty. With all the bins full of apples and an assortment of vegetables, it was a harvest that would make winter more secure.

Our garden was large, and all of us helped care for it. I did my weeding on a low stool after the sun went down. What wasn't eaten immediately was canned. Nothing was left for winter snow but dried vines and corn stubble. The best pumpkins were stored in the barn, and I always helped Mother prepare this fruit for pies. She would tie her big apron around my neck, as I liked hers better than mine. It gave me a feeling of being needed to be dressed like Mom.

Growing up in Scio County was having a playhouse with electricity and dimity curtains and serving a real tea; being cornered in the cornfield by Jupiter, the unfriendly bull; being a sleepy-eyed tot who tried to help Mother on Fridays with the dawn baking and the foolish little girl who throttled all the yellow baby chicks because she liked the black ones best. Growing up was experiencing the beauty of the sugar grove, the deer in the deep woods, the flowers in May, the turning leaves of autumn. Growing up was being allowed to meddle in Mother's kitchen—not only allowed, but encouraged—and Mother wiping away tears for failures and giving warning looks to the family when my first biscuits were served yellow and soda bitter.

Today as I write these words and live in the past again for just a little while, I pay tribute to Mother, who was my right hand in those early years. It was she who washed the endless stacks of pots and pans and took the words "I can't" from my vocabulary. I remember Mama's cookbook.

She had only one. It was covered in red checkered oilcloth and stood between two potted geraniums on the south windowsill. "One is all I need," she would say, "I keep everything in my head." Whenever we had company and long before I could read or write, I hoped to impress guests by peeking into the living room and importantly saying, "May I use your cookbook, Mother?"

I used to go exactly by a recipe, but later my flare for improvisation took me beyond the routine effort. As each new dish came to the table, my family courageously gave me their unbiased opinions. My crop of home-grown Henelys do the same thing today.

During modeling, a dancing career, and college, I still found time to cook and bake. As a TWA hostess and later when married, my travels brought me to some of the finest restaurants in Europe, Hawaii, and the Caribbean. Here I sought the secrets from the world's famous chefs. Sometimes it took persuasion and compliments when they reluctantly held back, and many times even a bribe was turned down. But more often my sincere admiration for their art took them by surprise, and I came away rewarded for my time and efforts with a menu filled with notes, or a recipe on a cocktail napkin.

In my kitchen hang three cooking diplomas which make me happy and proud. Any morning, if you wish, you may watch me cook and bake with the imported spices and distinctive recipes that are used today for the pleasure of those who dine in the Farmer's Daughter Restaurant.

Through the early years Mother and I worked together. Her patience and understanding became an inspiration that helped me fulfill a dream. It has taken years to complete and test all my recipes, but from this wide selection I have chosen my favorites: some from the growing years, some from the gadabout years, and some from today. All I am happy to share with you in the *Farmer's Daughter Cookbook*.

Stocks

BROWN STOCK

A must for good soups and sauces.

    4 lb. beef bones (neck preferred)
    1 gal. water
    2 tbsp. beef fat or margarine
    1⅓ C. sliced onion
    ⅔ C. chopped celery
    ⅔ C. chopped carrots
    2 C. crushed tomatoes
    Pinch of thyme
    ¼ tsp. crushed peppercorns
    2 whole cloves
    ½ bay leaf
    1 tbsp. fresh chopped parsley

Place bones in roasting pan. Brown in preheated oven (350°F.) turning occasionally. Add a small amount of water or beef stock to prevent burning toward the end. Place bones in soup pot. Place roasting pan over medium heat on top of stove until hot. Add 1 cup water. Scrape pan and put drippings and crust into soup pot. Add 1 gallon water and bring to boil. Simmer 3 hours. Sauté onion, celery, and carrots in margarine until light-colored. Add to soup pot with tomatoes and seasonings. Simmer 3 hours. Remove bones. Cool and refrigerate. Remove fat and reheat. Strain through cheesecloth. Clarify.* Refrigerate until ready to use. If you are going to store for more than 4 days, do not remove fat on top, as it aids in preserving the stock until ready to use.

HAM STOCK

Use as soup base.

1 ham bone
3 qt. cold water
2 carrots
4 stalks celery, cut in 1-inch pieces
1 bay leaf
½ tsp. crushed peppercorns
2 thinly sliced onions
2 tsp. salt

Combine all ingredients in 5-quart kettle. Heat to boiling point. Simmer 3 hours. Remove bone, clarify stock,* and strain. Keep in refrigerator.

* See *Index* under "Clarifying Stock."

WHITE STOCK

For soups and sauces.

5 lb. cracked veal knuckles (have your butcher do it)
4 qt. water
3 stalks celery (3-in. cuts)
2 carrots, sliced
1 onion, sliced
½ bay leaf
½ tsp. crushed peppercorns
1 tbsp. salt
2 tbsp. fresh chopped parsley
2 garlic cloves, cut up
2 sprigs thyme

Combine all ingredients in large kettle. Bring to boiling point. Simmer 5 hours. Strain and clarify.*

CLARIFYING STOCK

The method used for clearing basic stocks.

1 broken egg shell
1 egg white
¼ C. cold water
2 qt. hot stock

Mix egg white with cold water. Add to stock with broken shell. Bring to boiling point. Remove from heat. Let stand 5 minutes. Strain through double thickness of cheesecloth.

* See *Index* under "Clarifying Stock."

Soups and Chowders

BURNT OATMEAL SOUP

Nutritious and nourishing.

  1 C. rolled oats
  ½ C. ground carrots
  ½ C. ground onion
  ¼ C. ground celery
  ¼ bay leaf
  1 tsp. MSG
  2 cloves
  ¼ tsp. caraway seed
  2 juniper berries, crushed; or ¼ tsp. gin
  2 tbsp. chopped chives
  2 tbsp. chopped parsley
  1 tbsp. salt
  ⅛ tsp. ground fresh pepper
  2 qt. rich beef stock
  2 tbsp. butter

Brown oats in heavy skillet over low heat, stirring frequently. Add remaining ingredients to beef stock and bring to boil. Add oats. Simmer gently for 20 minutes. *Makes 2 quarts.*

CHEDDAR CHEESE SOUP

Farmer's Daughter favorite.

2 tsp. arrowroot
2 C. chicken stock
1 tbsp. chopped onion
¼ C. diced carrots
¼ C. diced celery
1 C. water
¼ C. butter
½ C. flour
3 C. hot milk
½ lb. sharp soft cheddar cheese, diced
½ tsp. salt
⅛ tsp. soda
¼ tsp. paprika
1 tsp. chopped fresh parsley
⅛ tsp. yellow food coloring

Dissolve arrowroot in ½ cup chicken stock. Cook onion, carrots, and celery in 1 cup water until tender. Melt butter. Add flour. Stir until smooth. Add 1½ cup chicken stock, arrowroot mixture, and cheese. Stir until cheese melts. Add milk, salt, soda, paprika, parsley, food coloring, vegetables, and water in which vegetables were cooked. Do not boil soup. *Serves 8.* If warmed up, a little milk may have to be added for the desired consistency.

CHICKEN BROTH

Alone or as a cream soup base.

    1 cut up chicken (3 to 4 lb.)
    2 qt. cold water
    1 carrot, sliced
    2 stalks celery
    ½ bay leaf
    ¼ tsp. crushed peppercorns
    1 onion, sliced
    1 tsp. salt
    ½ tsp. pepper

Combine all ingredients in 4- to 5-quart kettle. Simmer gently for 2 hours. Strain. *Makes 1 quart.* Use chicken in stews or soups.

CHICKEN CURRY SOUP

Bombay bisque.

    5 C. chicken broth
    ¾ C. chopped onion
    ¼ C. chopped leek
    ¾ C. chopped green pepper
    ¾ C. chopped celery
    1¾ C. chopped tomatoes
    ½ C. Minute rice
    1 tbsp. curry powder
    1½ C. chopped cooked ham
    2 tbsp. margarine
    2 tbsp. flour
    2 C. coffee cream

Combine broth and all vegetables in Dutch oven. Cook until tender. Add rice, curry powder, and ham. Cook covered 15 minutes. Melt margarine in saucepan. Add flour. Stir in coffee cream until thickened. Add to meat and vegetables. *Serves 8 to 10.*

CHICKEN VELVET SOUP

Truly is velvety.

   2 C. rich chicken stock
   1 tbsp. tapioca
   ¼ C. chicken fat
   ⅓ C. flour
   2 C. heavy cream
   3 C. milk
   2 tsp. salt
   ¼ tsp. white pepper
   1 tsp. MSG
   ¼ tsp. nutmeg
   1 tbsp. butter
   1 tsp. Worcestershire sauce

Bring chicken stock to boil. Add tapioca and cook until translucent. Melt chicken fat. Stir in flour. Cook until thickened. Add stock slowly with cream and milk. Add spices, butter, and Worcestershire sauce. Simmer 3 minutes. *Serves 6.*

CHILLED AVOCADO SOUP

For a hot summer soup-and-sandwich day.

   1 medium avocado
   1 C. coffee cream
   ½ C. commercial sour cream

1 C. clear chicken soup
Few drops onion juice
¼ tsp. salt
⅛ tsp. white pepper
Sour cream and chives for topping

Combine all ingredients except topping in blender. Beat until smooth. Chill 2 hours. Top each serving with a tea-spoon dollop of sour cream and a sprinkling of finely chopped chives. *Serves 4.*

CHILLED CUCUMBER SOUP

Cool and refreshing.

3 medium-size cucumbers
¼ C. butter
2 tbsp. flour
1 C. chicken broth
¾ tsp. salt
¼ tsp. white pepper
1½ C. coffee cream

Peel and cut cucumbers in half lengthwise and scoop out seeds. Cut in ⅓-inch pieces. Cover and sauté in butter until transparent. Remove cucumbers from pan. Stir flour into butter over medium heat. Gradually add broth, salt, and pepper, stirring constantly. Simmer 5 minutes. Put cucumbers and broth mixture into blender. Blend until smooth. Pour into bowl and add cream. Refrigerate until chilled, about 2 hours. Garnish with chopped chives or float a very thin slice of cucumber on top. *Serves 6.*

CREAM OF CARROT SOUP

A delicious idea from the Amish.

¼ C. chicken fat
¼ C. all-purpose flour
1 C. cooked, ground carrots
1 C. carrot liquor
2 C. chicken stock
1 C. coffee cream
1½ tsp. salt
⅛ tsp. white pepper
¼ tsp. celery salt
¼ tsp. Worcestershire sauce
½ tsp. MSG.
Pinch cayenne

Melt chicken fat. Stir in flour. Combine carrot liquor, stock, and cream. Add to flour mixture and cook until thickened. Add seasonings, Worcestershire sauce, and carrots. Cook over low heat 5 minutes. *Serves 6 to 8.* If warmed up, you may have to add a little milk for the desired consistency.

CREAM OF LEEK SOUP

We gathered the leeks in the woods.

2 C. chicken broth
½ C. minced leek

¼ C. minced onion
1 C. diced potatoes
½ tsp. salt
¼ tsp. white pepper
Pinch of cayenne
3 tbsp. tapioca
2½ C. milk
1 tbsp. butter
1 C. coffee cream

Simmer leeks, onion, and potatoes in chicken broth until tender. Add seasoning, tapioca, milk, and butter. Simmer ½ hour. Add cream and reheat. Do not boil. Season to taste. *Serves 6.*

CREAM OF LETTUCE SOUP

A delicate color and flavor.

¼ C. melted butter
⅓ C. all-purpose flour
½ C. chopped outer leaves of lettuce
3 C. hot chicken broth
1 C. coffee cream
½ C. cut up lettuce (½-inch pieces)
1 tsp. salt
¼ tsp. white pepper

Braise outer leaves of lettuce in butter. Strain. Add flour to butter. Combine chicken broth and cream. Add to flour mixture and stir. Cook until thickened. Add salt, pepper, and cut up lettuce. Cook 5 minutes. Do not boil. If reheated, you may have to add a little milk for the desired consistency.

CREAM OF PARSLEY SOUP

A lowly garnish gets top billing.

1 C. finely chopped fresh parsley
3 C. rich chicken stock
2 C. coffee cream
2 egg yolks
½ tsp. salt
Dash cayenne pepper

Bring parsley and chicken stock to boil. Simmer for 20 minutes. Beat cream, egg yolks, salt, and pepper for 1 minute. Add to stock, and stir over low heat 3 minutes. *Serves 6.*

CREAM OF PECAN SOUP

Good finale for a Louisiana crop.

1 C. finely ground pecans
1 qt. beef stock
1 tsp. finely chopped parsley
2 tbsp. finely chopped onion
½ tsp. celery salt
⅛ tsp. nutmeg
2 C. coffee cream

Combine pecans, stock, parsley, onion, celery, salt, and nutmeg. Bring to a boil and simmer 10 minutes. Add cream and reheat. Do not boil. *Serves 6 to 8.*

CREAM OF TOMATO AND MUSHROOM SOUP

Added ingredients lift the flavor.

 ½ C. chopped canned mushrooms*
 1 tbsp. chopped onions
 ¼ C. margarine or chicken fat
 ¼ C. all-purpose flour
 2 C. milk
 1¼ C. chicken stock
 ¼ tsp. sugar
 ¼ tsp. salt
 ⅛ tsp. black pepper
 ¾ C. tomato purée
 1 C. heavy cream
 ¼ tsp. soda

Sauté mushrooms and onions in margarine. Stir in flour. Add milk and chicken stock slowly while stirring. Add sugar, salt, black pepper, tomato purée, and heat to simmer. Stir in cream and soda, and continue to cook until foam disappears. *Serves 6 to 8.*

DANISH CHICKEN SOUP

First course to a smorgasbord.

 ¼ C. chicken fat
 ¼ C. all-purpose flour
 4 C. hot chicken stock
 1½ C. coffee cream
 ¾ C. diced cooked chicken
 ¼ C. diced cooked celery
 Pinch of nutmeg
 ⅛ tsp. celery salt
 1½ tsp. salt

* Fresh mushrooms may be used instead.

½ tsp. white pepper
¼ tsp. Worcestershire sauce
1 C. spaetzels

Melt chicken fat. Stir in flour. Combine stock with
cream. Add to flour mixture and cook until thickened. Add
chicken, celery, seasonings, and spaetzels. *Serves 8.*

DOWN EAST OYSTER STEW

A light supper.

18 oysters
½ C. butter
¼ tsp. Worcestershire sauce
Dash cayenne
Dash celery salt
1 qt. coffee cream
1 tsp. salt
½ tsp. fresh, chopped parsley
¼ tsp. white pepper

Sauté oysters in butter just until sides curl. Add remaining ingredients. Heat to simmering point. Pour into individual bowls and sprinkle with paprika, if desired. *Serves 4.*

FARMER'S BREAD SOUP

For a penny budget with epicurean flavor.

½ bay leaf
2 whole cloves
½ tsp. whole caraway seed
¾ C. finely ground hard potato bread
¾ C. finely chopped onion
1 tsp. salt
¼ tsp. pepper
2 tbsp. fresh chopped parsley
1½ qt. rich beef stock
2 tbsp. butter

Place bay leaf, cloves, and caraway seed in small cheese-cloth bag and put in 3-quart soup pot. Mix all ingredients in the soup pot and bring to a boil. Simmer 10 minutes. Remove spice bag. *Serves 8 to 10.*

FRENCH MARKET ONION SOUP

Down by the Marseilles wharf.

3 C. thinly sliced onion
2 tbsp. beef fat or margarine
5 C. rich beef stock
¼ tsp. caramel coloring
½ tsp. salt
6 small slices of Italian bread, toasted
6 slices Gruyère cheese

Sauté onions over low heat in beef fat or margarine until golden brown and caramelized, stirring occasionally. Add stock, salt, and caramel coloring. Simmer 20 minutes. Pour into individual heat-proof crockery soup bowls. Garnish with a slice of Italian toasted bread and topped with Gruyère cheese. Place under broiler until cheese is soft and bubbly. *Serves 6.*

GARDEN PEA SOUP

Pick them in June.

2 C. fresh peas
2½ C. chicken stock
1½ C. warm coffee cream
2 tbsp. minced onion
¼ C. butter
¼ C. flour
1 tsp. salt
⅛ tsp. white pepper
½ tsp. MSG.

Cook peas in chicken stock until tender. Drain and mash ½ of the peas and return to the stock. Sauté onion in butter until transparent. Stir in flour. Add milk, stock, and mashed peas. Simmer 5 minutes. Add remaining peas. *Serves 6.*

LANCASTER RED BEAN SOUP

Thick and hearty.

2 tbsp. bacon fat
¼ C. chopped onion
¼ C. chopped celery
½ tsp. salt
Dash of hot sauce
¼ C. whole canned kidney beans
¼ C. mashed kidney beans
3 C. beef broth
½ C. cooked rice

Sauté onion and celery in bacon fat. Add remainder of ingredients. Bring to a boil and simmer 10 minutes. *Serves 4.*

MAINE COAST CLAM CHOWDER

It is worth the trouble.

1 tbsp. margarine
2 tbsp. diced salt pork

1 garlic clove, minced
1 C. chopped onion

Sauté and cook until tender. Add:

¼ C. chopped green pepper
¼ C. chopped celery
2 tsp. salt
¼ C. diced carrots
2 C. diced potatoes
6 C. boiling water

Cover and bring to boil. Reduce heat and cook 10 minutes. Add:

1½ C. crushed tomatoes
1 C. clams
¼ tsp. pepper
½ C. clam juice
1 bay leaf
4 whole cloves
1 tsp. sugar
2 tsp. butter
½ tsp. thyme
⅓ C. chopped parsley
1 tsp. Worcestershire sauce
¾ C. tomato catsup
¼ tsp. paprika
1 tsp. tapioca

Simmer ½ hour. Remove bay leaf and cloves. *Serves 8.*

MULLIGATAWNY SOUP

You can't beat the Dutch in Pennsylvania.

¼ C. chopped carrots
¼ C. chopped celery

¼ C. chopped turnip
¼ C. chopped onion
2½ qt. beef stock
½ C. margarine
½ C. flour
⅛ tsp. curry powder
1 tsp. fresh chopped parsley
⅛ tsp. ground cloves
Pinch of mace
1 tsp. salt
½ bay leaf
1 tbsp. lemon juice
1 tsp. Worcestershire sauce
½ C. peeled and chopped apple
¼ C. sliced canned mushrooms
¾ C. diced meat (chicken, veal, ham, or beef)
½ C. cooked rice

Cook carrots, celery, turnips, and onions in 2 cups beef stock until tender. Strain and reserve stock and vegetables separately. Melt margarine. Stir in flour. Add beef stock and cook until thickened. Add remaining ingredients. Simmer ½ hour. *Serves 10 to 12.*

NEW ENGLAND CLAM CHOWDER

Coastal cooks can dig for their supper.

1 C. diced potatoes
1½ C. cold water
3 tbsp. ground salt pork
¼ C. chopped onion
½ C. all-purpose flour
2 C. clam juice
1 C. hot milk
1 C. coffee cream

1 tsp. salt
½ tsp. white pepper
½ tsp. Worcestershire sauce
1 C. clams
2 tbsp. butter

Cook potatoes in water until tender. Strain and save the water and potatoes separately. Place salt pork in soup pot. Cook until partially rendered. Add onions and sauté. Stir in flour. Add clam juice and potato water. Stir until smooth and thick. Add milk and cream. Bring to simmer point, stirring constantly. Add salt, pepper, Worcestershire sauce, clams, potatoes, and butter. *Serves 6 to 8.*

SPANISH COLD VEGETABLE SOUP

Salud, Madrid!

SOUP INGREDIENTS
2 C. canned tomatoes
5 garlic cloves, cut up
2 tsp. salt
¼ tsp. black pepper
2 tbsp. paprika
2 tsp. sugar
3 C. peeled, chopped cucumber
Dash of cayenne
Dash of tabasco sauce
⅓ C. olive oil
3 tbsp. white vinegar
3 tbsp. chopped onion
½ C. chopped green pepper
2 C. tomato purée
1½ qt. cold clear chicken broth

GARNISHES

½ C. chopped onion
½ C. fresh chopped tomato
½ C. croutons
½ C. chopped green pepper
½ C. chopped cucumber

Blend all ingredients except tomato purée and chicken broth in blender. Chill thoroughly. Add chicken broth and purée. Serve in large bowls. Pass separate small bowls of garnish to the guests. *Serves 10* at your next Spanish dinner party.

TANGERINE SOUP

You won't believe how the ingredients mate!

5 C. rich chicken stock
1 C. tangerine juice
1 C. diced, cooked chicken, white meat
½ C. bamboo shoots
¼ C. chopped green onion with tops
2 tbsp. chopped, cooked ham
1 tsp. salt
½ tsp. MSG.
2 C. cubed honeydew melon
1 C. tangerine sections, free of seeds and membrane
2 tbsp. finely chopped pistachio nuts for garnish

Combine all ingredients in saucepan. Heat to boiling point. Serve in bowls. Garnish with pistachio nuts. *Serves 8.*

TOMATO BISQUE

Carolina plantation fare.

2 C. chicken broth
¼ C. diced celery
¼ C. sliced carrots
¼ C. chopped onion
¼ C. chicken fat
¼ C. flour
1 C. warmed milk
1¼ C. warmed heavy cream
1 tsp. salt
¼ tsp. soda
½ tsp. black pepper
⅔ C. crushed canned tomatoes
⅓ C. diced fresh tomatoes
1 tbsp. sugar
2 tbsp. butter

Cook celery, carrots, and onion in chicken broth. Strain and reserve the broth and vegetables separately. Melt chicken fat. Stir in flour. Add broth slowly and cook until thickened. Add milk, cream, salt, and soda. Simmer gently 5 minutes. Add cooked vegetables, crushed tomatoes, fresh tomatoes, sugar, and butter. Cook 3 minutes. *Serves 6.*

TURKEY VEGETABLE SOUP

Save that carcass.

1 turkey carcass, broken into large pieces
4 qt. water
2¼ C. crushed tomatoes
½ C. diced celery
¾ C. diced onion

1 tbsp. chicken base
½ tsp. poultry seasoning
¼ tsp. black pepper
½ tsp. salt
1 tbsp. tapioca
⅔ C. uncooked rice
1 package (12 oz.) mixed frozen vegetables

Put carcass in large soup kettle with water. Simmer 2 hours. Remove carcass and take off meat. Cut in bite-size pieces. Put meat back in kettle with tomatoes, celery, onion, chicken base, and seasonings. Cover and bring to boil. Reduce heat and simmer ½ hour. Add tapioca, rice, and vegetables. Cook ½ hour. Cool and refrigerate 4 hours. Remove fat that has formed on top of soup. Reheat. *Serves 8 to 10.*

WINTER CORN SOUP

Soup and sandwich idea.

⅓ C. chicken fat
½ C. flour
2 C. coffee cream
5 C. milk
2 C. cream-style corn
1 tsp. sugar
¼ tsp. celery salt
1½ tsp. salt
¾ tsp. white pepper
Pinch of cayenne

Melt chicken fat. Stir in flour. Add cream and milk. Stir until thickened. Add corn, sugar, and spices. Simmer 3 minutes. *Serves 6 to 8.*

Vegetables

I suppose I began to read in the primary grades just as all children do, but I don't remember a time that I couldn't identify words such as broccoli, kohlrabi, and zucchini— either on the seed packets we staked beside the plantings or on the jars on the cellar shelf. And perhaps my vision is too rosy in retrospect, but I cannot recall any "I don't want" phrases coming from the little ones sitting at our dinner table.

We relished all the green, root, and stem vegetables even though the seasons brought favorites. There was no dreariness in our vegetable menu; a repetition need not occur for a week or more if Mama chose, and then she would never be at a loss to vary the vegetable with lemon butter, cream sauce, or baked with crumbs. There were very few vegetables that Mama thought couldn't be sliced for a raw relish tray.

From spring asparagus until the last potato was dug in November, our vegetables grew in a well-tended and well-loved plot in view of the kitchen window. We picked our vegetables just after nap time, and I recall the pride of being given the willow basket and sent for our supper. Or sometimes Mama would say, "Pick your favorite because you have been such a help to me today."

AU GRATIN POTATOES

Make them ahead, and bake when needed.

POTATOES
1½ qt. diced, cooked potatoes
¾ qt. cheese sauce
1 tsp. salt

TOPPING
¼ c. ground cheddar cheese
¼ c. fresh bread crumbs

Mix all ingredients except topping, thoroughly. Put in 2½ qt. greased casserole dish. Sprinkle topping over potato mixture and brown in preheated oven (350°F.) for 30 minutes. Slide under broiler for 3 minutes. *Serves 10.*

CARROT CURLICUES

A vegetable garnish for pretty platters.

Scrape carrots. Slice thin with vegetable cutter. Roll and fasten with toothpick. Place in ice water for 1 hour. Use to decorate or brown them in the oven, basting with butter. Remove toothpick before serving.

COMPANY SPINACH MOLDS

For the boss's next invitation.

2 packages (10 oz.) frozen chopped spinach
6 eggs, slightly beaten
1 C. finely grated onion
¼ tsp. white pepper
¼ tsp. dried savory
3 tbsp. butter, melted
1⅓ C. milk
1 tbsp. white vinegar
1¼ tsp. salt
8 tomato slices, each 2½ x ⅓ inches

Cook spinach as label directs, but do not add salt.
Drain. In medium bowl combine butter, spinach, eggs,
milk, onions, salt, pepper, vinegar, and savory. Butter 8-
or 9-ounce custard cups. Divide spinach mixture into
each. Place cups in shallow pan with 1 inch of hot water
in it. Bake in preheated oven (350°F.) for 35 to 40 minutes or until custard is set. Remove from oven and unmold
onto hot tomato slices which have been sprinkled with salt
and black ground pepper. *Serves 8 to 10.* Can be made the
day before.

DUCHESSE POTATOES

A border to rim the plank.

2 egg yolks, beaten slightly
3 C. hot mashed potatoes
Dash of paprika
3 tbsp. butter
¾ tsp. salt
½ tsp. white pepper

⅛ tsp. garlic salt
1 tbsp. chopped chives or finely chopped onion

Blend all ingredients. Shape into mounds on greased cookie sheet or use for border of planked steak and casseroles. Brush with Egg Yolk Glaze.* Brown in oven preheated to 450°F.

FARM FRIED POTATOES

Will satisfy harvest hand appetites.

Boil potatoes with jackets to firm stage. Cool. Peel. Slice thin. Fry in lard. Salt as desired. Turn when crisp.

FRENCH FRIED ONION RINGS

For humdinger hamburgers.

1 C. sifted all-purpose flour
¼ C. cornstarch
¼ C. salad oil
1 C. milk, scant
½ tsp. salt
⅛ tsp. yellow food coloring
Spanish or Bermuda onions, cut in ⅓-inch rings

Mix all ingredients except onions. Beat 2 minutes. Dip onion rings into batter. Let drip. Fry in hot fat about 2 to 3 minutes, turning once. Drain and salt immediately. *Makes about 2½ cups batter.*

* See *Index.*

ITALIAN FRIED PARSLEY

A delicious eatable garnish.

Wash sprigs of parsley. Dry thoroughly by shaking on a towel or air dry in parsley basket. Fry in deep fat (375°F.) for 1 minute. Sprinkle with salt and pepper. Use as an entrée garnish.

JULIA'S SAUERKRAUT
Spice it up!

    5 slices bacon, cut up with scissors
    1 C. chopped onion
    1 tbsp. flour
    2½ C. sauerkraut
    2 cloves garlic, crushed
    ½ tsp. caraway seed
    ½ C. white wine
    Water

Fry bacon. Remove from pan and set aside. Add onions to drippings. Stir in flour. Brown slightly. Add washed sauerkraut. Add seasonings and wine. Cover with water. Simmer 1½ hours. Serve with beef. Variation: Add ¼ cup dry mushrooms after covering sauerkraut with water.

ORANGE CANDIED SWEET POTATOES

Make it on the holidays.

    6 medium sweet potatoes, baked
    ¼ C. butter
    2 tbsp. orange juice
    ½ tbsp. grated orange peel
    ½ C. light corn syrup
    1 orange, cut in slices
    ¼ C. brown sugar, packed

Pare and halve sweet potatoes. Melt butter in skillet.
Add potatoes. Combine remaining ingredients. Pour over
potatoes. Cook uncovered over low heat until glazed.
Baste frequently. *Serves 6.*

POTATO FLAT CAKES

Another way to use up your leftover mashed potatoes.

    3 C. leftover mashed potatoes
    1 egg, beaten
    ½ tsp. salt
    ¼ tsp. white pepper

Mix all ingredients. Shape into flat cakes ¾ inch thick.
Drop onto hot griddle that has been greased with lard.
Turn with pancake turner when brown. *Makes approxi-
mately 6 to 8 flat cakes.*

POTATO PANCAKES

The secret in keeping them white is in adding ascorbic acid.

4 eggs
⅔ C. sifted all-purpose flour
1½ tsp. salt
½ tsp. white pepper
⅛ tsp. baking powder
2 tbsp. bacon drippings
2 tbsp. chopped bacon
½ C. milk
½ C. finely chopped onion
5 C. grated raw potatoes
1 tsp. ascorbic acid (fruit acid)

Beat eggs in mixer until fluffy. Stir in remaining ingredients. Using a ⅓-cup measure, drop batter onto hot griddle. Turn once. Do not stack pancakes. May be sprinkled with bacon bits and served with hot applesauce. *Makes 14 pancakes (5 inch).*

POTATO PUFFS

Another mashed potato variation.

2 C. mashed potatoes
1 egg, beaten
½ tsp. salt
⅛ tsp. pepper
1 tsp, fresh parsley, chopped

Combine all ingredients until well mixed. Flour hands and roll in 1-inch balls. Deep fry (375°F.) until brown. Drain. Serve hot. *Makes approximately 16 to 20 balls.* Variation: One-fourth cup grated cheese or ¼ cup finely chopped onion may be mixed with the potatoes.

ROAST POTATOES

Perfect partners with roast beef.

Pare medium potatoes. Cook in boiling, salted water for 15 minutes. Drain. With this short precook in water, potatoes will be done when roast is ready. About 1 hour before roast is done, place hot potatoes in the meat drippings around the roast. Baste potatoes frequently. Sprinkle lightly with salt before serving.

STEWED TOMATOES WITH CELERY

Choose the bright red ones.

    3 C. fresh tomatoes
    ⅔ C. fresh diced celery
    ½ C. water
    1¼ tsp. salt
    ½ tsp. sugar
    2 tsp. butter
    ⅛ tsp. pepper

Remove stem ends from washed tomatoes. Peel and cut into small pieces. Cook celery in water until tender. Drain. Add tomatoes, salt, sugar, butter, and pepper. Cover and heat to boiling. Reduce heat and simmer gently 8 to 10 minutes. *Serves 6 to 8.*

SWEET-SOUR CABBAGE

Cook it the day before.

1 C. finely chopped onion
¼ C. chicken fat
1 C. chopped apple
¼ C. crushed pineapple
6 C. shredded red cabbage
1 C. water
Pinch of cloves
Dash of cinnamon
½ bay leaf
2 tsp. salt
½ tsp. pepper
2 tsp. caraway seed
⅓ C. red wine vinegar
¼ C. Burgundy wine

Sauté onion in chicken fat until transparent. Add remaining ingredients. Stir and cover. Cook gently 1½
hours. Reheat the next day. *Serves 6 to 8.*

TO SAUTÉ LARGE MUSHROOMS

Tiny pinwheels to enhance a steak.

Wipe mushrooms with a damp cloth. Cut off stem even
with cap. Cut grooves in top of cap to obtain pinwheel
effect: Starting near center, cut ⅛ inch deep toward outer
edge of cap, make a second cut close and parallel to the
first cut, and lift out this narrow strip. Space cuts evenly
around the cap of the mushroom, approximately ½ inch
apart. Sauté in margarine, cooking slowly and turning gently, until lightly browned. Sprinkle with salt and pepper.
Serve hot.

TOMATO-RICE CASSEROLE

Serve with meat balls or veal cutlets.

1¾ C. uncooked rice
⅓ C. chopped onion
¼ C. chopped green pepper
¼ C. salad oil
2¼ C. beef broth
3¼ C. crushed canned tomatoes
1½ tsp. salt
1 tsp. pepper
1 tsp. MSG.
Dash chili powder

Sauté rice, onion, and green pepper in salad oil until delicately brown. Add remaining ingredients and cook over low heat until liquid is absorbed, approximately 25 minutes. To serve, put in a lightly greased 2-quart casserole.

YORKSHIRE POTATO PIE

A company favorite.

6 medium potatoes
⅓ C. milk
1 bouillon cube
3 tbsp. butter
1 tsp. salt
¼ tsp. white pepper
1 egg, slightly beaten
1 egg yolk (for brushing top of potatoes)
½ tsp. paprika

Boil and mash potatoes. Dissolve bouillon in hot milk. Add butter, salt, pepper, and egg. Beat. Pour mixture into potatoes and mix well. Pile into greased oven-glass pie dish (8 inch). Smooth top with knife. Brush with beaten egg yolk. Sprinkle with paprika. Brown in oven (400°F.) approximately 15 to 20 minutes. *Serves 6 to 8.*

Meats

In upstate New York where our farmland lay, we children usually suggested the sweets; Mama planned the vegetables and salads dependent upon her in-season garden produce or her home-canned supplies. But Papa was the meat provider. His smokehouse and salting sheds were as meticulously manned as a government-inspected shop is today. His aged meats were tagged and dated and checked daily.

I was never up early enough to join Papa at his before–sun-up breakfast, but it was then that he and Mama would decide what he would bring in later for our supper. Fresh chickens, sweet ham, or a ten-inch cut of a prime rib could be on our dinner menu. Mama ground her own meats for patties or meat loaf; made her own marinades for pot roasts and stews; and needed no blue stamping to tell her our meat was prime. We were encouraged to have large portions—Papa always said, "Good meat will tell in your bones."

BARBECUED BACK RIBS

Spareribs may be used.

4 lb. back ribs
1 recipe Barbecue Sauce*

Arrange ribs in shallow pan. Broil until brown on both sides. Pour off fat. Pour Barbecue Sauce over ribs. Place in 350°F. preheated oven. Bake approximately 1 hour. Baste occasionally. *Serves 4.*

BEEF BALLS

For broth soups.

½ lb. ground beef
2 tbsp. milk
¼ C. minced onion
¼ tsp. black pepper
¼ tsp. salt
¼ C. commercial bread crumbs
1 egg, beaten
1 qt. chicken broth

Mix together all ingredients except broth. Form into small ½-inch balls. Drop into boiling chicken broth. Simmer 10 minutes. Lift balls out and drain. *Makes approximately 25 balls.*

* See *Index.*

BEEF LOAF

Make ahead for busy days!

LOAF
4 slices hard bread
1 C. hot milk
1 lb. ground beef
1 lb. ground veal
¼ lb. ground pork
1 tbsp. Worcestershire sauce
¾ C. chopped onion
1 tbsp. chopped green pepper
1 tbsp. chopped celery
½ tsp. pepper
1 tsp. salt
2 eggs, beaten
½ C. boiling water

SAUCE
¾ C. tomato sauce
¼ C. beef broth
1 tbsp. finely chopped fresh parsley

Soak bread in hot milk for 5 minutes. Mix all remaining loaf ingredients and add bread and milk. Shape in greased loaf pan (9 x 5 x 2 inches). Refrigerate overnight. Bake in preheated oven (350°F.) for approximately 1½ hours. Heat tomato sauce and beef broth. Pour over meat loaf on serving platter. Garnish with parsley. *Serves 8.*

BEEF STROGANOFF

Serve with rice or noodles.

¼ C. flour
1 tsp. salt
¼ tsp. pepper
2 lb. lean beef round, ½ inch thick
2 tbsp. margarine
¾ C. sliced onion
1 garlic clove, minced
1 beef bouillon cube
2 C. boiling water
1 can button mushrooms (4 oz.)
1 tsp. Worcestershire sauce
2 tbsp. tomato sauce
⅔ C. sour cream
2 tsp. white vinegar
1 tbsp. fresh chopped parsley

Combine flour, salt, and pepper. Trim meat and cut in strips 1½ x 3 inches. Coat with flour-seasoning mixture. Melt margarine in heavy skillet. Brown meat on all sides. Add onion and garlic. Dissolve bouillon cube in boiling water and add to meat. Add liquid from mushrooms, Worcestershire sauce, and tomato sauce. Cover and simmer until meat is tender, about 1½ hours. Add mushrooms. Just before serving combine vinegar with sour cream, and stir in. Heat but do not boil. Top with parsley. *Serves 6.*

BURGUNDY CUBED STEAKS

Silk-purse steaks.

8 cubed steaks
2 tbsp. salad oil
½ C. catsup

½ C. water
1½ tsp. sugar
2 tbsp. chopped onion
½ tsp. chili powder
½ tsp. Worcestershire sauce
1 tbsp. chopped fresh parsley
½ C. canned button mushrooms

Brown steaks on both sides in hot salad oil. Combine
remaining ingredients. Pour over steaks. Cover and simmer 40 minutes or until tender. Serve with rice. *Serves 8.*

CHILI CON CARNE

For a frosty eve.

¼ C. chopped onion
3 tbsp. beef fat
½ C. chopped celery
¼ C. chopped green pepper
1 lb. coarsely ground beef
1 garlic clove, minced
1¾ tsp. salt
Dash of cayenne pepper
2¼ C. tomatoes, crushed
½ C. beef stock
1¼ C. pinto beans, drained
Dash of tabasco sauce
2 tsp. chili powder
2 tbsp. hot water
½ C. canned button mushrooms

Sauté onion in hot fat until transparent. Add celery,
green pepper, and meat. Cook approximately 10 minutes
or until meat is almost done. Add garlic, salt, cayenne,
tomatoes, beef stock, beans, and tabasco sauce. Cover

and heat to boiling. Simmer 15 minutes, stirring occasionally. Blend chili powder and hot water. Stir into mixture. Add mushrooms. Cook 5 minutes. *Serves 6.* Make it the day before. Freezes well.

COMPANY VEAL LOAF

Guest dish for the low budget.

    2 lb. ground veal
    ¼ lb. ground pork
    2½ tsp. salt
    ¼ tsp. pepper
    1 egg, beaten
    1 C. milk
    1 C. ground cracker crumbs
    3 tbsp. minced onion
    2 tbsp. lemon juice
    5 C. hot mashed potatoes

Mix all ingredients except potatoes. Pack in greased loaf pan. Bake in preheated oven (325°F.) for 1½ hours. Turn out onto heated platter. Frost with mashed potatoes and make a design by drawing a knife broadside across the top of the loaf. Sprinkle with paprika. Return to oven for 20 minutes. Pan gravy may be made from the drippings.* *Serves 10 to 12.*

COUNTRY HOUSE STEW

Made to be warmed up the following day.

    FIRST DAY
    2 lb. beef chuck, cut in chunks
    3 tbsp. flour
    2 tbsp. beef fat

* See *Index.*

4 C. hot beef stock
2 tsp. lemon juice
1 tsp. Worcestershire sauce
1 garlic clove, minced
¾ C. sliced onion
½ bay leaf
1 tbsp. salt
1 tsp. black pepper
½ tsp. paprika
1 tsp. sugar
1 tbsp. chopped fresh parsley
Dash of thyme
Dash of allspice
¼ C. red wine
2 C. crushed canned tomatoes
½ C. tomato paste
1 tsp. gravy master
1 tsp. tapioca

SECOND DAY
3 carrots, cut in chunks
8 small onions
6 small potatoes, peeled
3 stalks celery, cut in chunks
4 C. beef stock

First Day: Dust meat with flour. Brown meat on all sides in beef fat in Dutch oven. Add all first day ingredients and simmer 1 hour; remove bay leaf. Let cool and refrigerate overnight.

Second Day: Reheat to simmer. Cook vegetables in beef stock until tender; add to meat. *Serves 6 to 8.*

COUNTRY POT ROAST

Ready for Sunday.

    4 lb. beef pot roast
    ½ tsp. ground black pepper
    ⅛ tsp. ground cloves
    ⅛ tsp. mace
    ⅛ tsp. allspice
    1 tbsp. salt
    1 C. chopped onion
    2 tbsp. lemon juice
    ½ garlic clove, minced
    ½ C. salad oil
    2 tbsp. wine vinegar
    1½ C. tomato juice
    2 bay leaves
    6 small peeled tomatoes

Wipe meat with damp cloth. Mix dry ingredients and rub into meat. Add remaining ingredients to meat, using only ¼ cup salad oil. Marinate in refrigerator overnight, turning occasionally. When ready to use, take meat out and sprinkle with flour. Brown meat in the remaining ¼ cup salad oil. Add the marinade and cover roast. Roast in preheated oven (325°F.) approximately 3 hours or until tender. Make pan gravy from drippings.*

* See *Index*.

DAD'S GREEN PEPPERS

His kitchen specialty when the girls were busy.

    2 lb. ground beef
    ½ lb. ground pork
    1 C. rice
    1 C. chopped onion
    1 egg
    1½ tsp. salt
    ½ tsp. pepper
    ¼ tsp. thyme
    ¼ tsp. mixed herbs
    ¼ C. canned mushrooms
    2 tbsp. chopped fresh parsley
    8 large green peppers
    4 C. crushed canned tomatoes
    2 C. tomato purée

Combine all ingredients except peppers, tomatoes, and
purée. Wash peppers and cut tops. Remove membrane
and seeds. Fill peppers loosely. Put in large kettle. Pour
tomatoes and purée over peppers. Cover and simmer 1
hour. Remove cover and continue to simmer ½ hour.
Cool and refrigerate. Reheat and use the next day.

HAM LOAF

Rich and peachy good.

    1½ lb. ground smoked ham
    1 lb. ground pork
    1 C. bread crumbs
    ½ C. chopped onion
    2 eggs, beaten
    1 C. milk
    8 canned peach halves

⅓ C. margarine
⅓ C. brown sugar, packed

Combine all ingredients. Pack in oblong baking dish (2 quart). Bake in preheated oven (350°F.) for 1 hour. Melt margarine. Add brown sugar. Baste peach halves. Arrange peach halves on ham loaf and pour sauce mixture over top. Continue to bake ½ hour more. *Serves 10 to 12.*

HAMBURGER POTATO PIE

A quickie.

3/4 C. chopped onion
2 tbsp. margarine
1½ lb. ground beef
1 tsp. salt
½ tsp. pepper
1 C. cooked, drained peas
1¾ C. crushed, canned tomatoes
⅔ C. catsup
3 C. hot mashed potatoes
1 egg, beaten

Sauté onion in margarine. Add meat and seasonings. Cook until meat is lightly browned. Add peas, tomatoes, and catsup. Mix well. Pour into greased casserole (2 quart). Combine mashed potatoes and egg. Spoon mounds of potatoes onto meat mixture. Bake in preheated oven (350° F.) for 20 to 30 minutes.

ITALIAN MEATBALLS

Good with spaghetti.

1 lb. ground beef
½ lb. ground pork
½ C. minced onion
¾ C. dry bread crumbs
1 tbsp. minced parsley
1½ tsp. salt
⅛ tsp. pepper
1 tsp. Worcestershire sauce
1 egg
½ C. milk
1 tsp. paprika
1 garlic clove, minced
2 tbsp. Parmesan cheese

Mix all ingredients together. Shape into 1-inch balls.
Brown in ¼ cup hot salad oil. Place meatballs in Spaghetti Sauce.*

MEATBALLS IN BLANKETS

Tasty tidbits for a cocktail party.

1 C. ground cooked meat, beef, pork, or veal
¼ C. milk
1 egg, beaten
½ C. grated cheddar cheese
½ C. commercial bread crumbs
2 tbsp. lemon juice
2 tbsp. finely chopped green pepper
2 tbsp. thinly sliced olives
1 tbsp. minced pimento

* See *Index*.

¼ C. minced onion
½ tsp. salt
¼ tsp. pepper
Flour
12 strips bacon, cut in halves

Mix well all ingredients except bacon. Form in 1-inch balls or cylindrical shapes. Pat with flour. Wrap each in bacon and fasten with toothpick. Deep fry (350°F.) until bacon is crisp. *Makes 24.*

OXTAIL STEW

An entire meal with a green salad.

4 lb. oxtails
1 tsp. salt
½ tsp. white pepper
3 tbsp. margarine
2 qt. beef stock
2 tbsp. sugar
1 C. crushed tomatoes
¼ C. tapioca
½ C. tomato pieces
1 clove garlic, pressed
3 C. cooked, diced potatoes
1 C. cooked, diced carrots
1 C. cooked, sliced onions
⅓ C. good red Burgundy wine

Wash oxtails and dry with a towel. Season with salt and pepper. Sauté in Dutch oven with margarine until brown. Add beef stock, sugar, tomatoes, tapioca, tomato pieces, and garlic. Cover and simmer 2 hours. Add vegetables. Cool and refrigerate 4 hours. Skim off fat and reheat. Add wine. *Serves 8.*

ROUND STEAK CHUNKS

Noodles and I.

    2 lb. round steak, cut in bite-size chunks
    2 tbsp. flour
    3 tbsp. beef fat
    1 C. chopped onion
    1 tbsp. salt
    ½ tsp. pepper
    1 tsp. paprika
    2 garlic cloves, minced
    1 C. dry mushrooms
    1½ C. undiluted canned tomato soup
    ½ C. water
    2 C. commercial sour cream

Flour steak chunks. Sauté onion and steak in beef fat.
Add remaining ingredients except sour cream. Simmer
1½ hours or until tender. Add sour cream and reheat.
Serve on bed of green noodles.

RUMP ROAST

Sunday dinner and next-day lean slices.

    4- to 5-lb. beef rump, rolled
    2 tbsp. vegetable shortening
    ⅓ C. cider vinegar
    1½ tsp. salt
    ½ tsp. pepper
    1 garlic clove, cut up
    ½ C. water

Heat shortening in large skillet. Brown roast on all
sides. Mix the remaining ingredients and pour over roast.

Roast in preheated oven (350°F.) for about 2 to 3 hours or until tender. Baste frequently with drippings. Serve with Zippy Chili Sauce.* *Serves 10 to 12.*

SIRLOIN BURGER

A glorious burger.

BURGER
2 lb. sirloin of beef, ground
1 egg, beaten slightly
1 C. cool chicken broth
¼ tsp. dry mustard
1½ tsp. salt
½ tsp. black pepper
2 tbsp. Worcestershire sauce
½ tsp. MSG

SAUCE
1½ C. Brown Sauce* or commercial beef gravy
½ tsp. dry mustard
2 tsp. A-1 steak sauce
½ C. catsup
2 tbsp. butter
1 tbsp. chopped fresh parsley

Mix all burger ingredients. Shape into 8 to 10 patties. Fry in 1 tablespoon salad oil until the desired doneness. In a saucepan, mix all sauce ingredients. Heat to simmer. Pour sauce over burgers. *Serves 8.*

* See *Index.*

STROGANOFF HAMBURGERS

The shopping day dinner.

    8 hamburger patties
    2 tbsp. salad oil
    1 C. canned mushroom soup
    ¼ C. canned mushrooms
    ¼ C. mushroom liquor
    1 C. sour cream
    1 tbsp. fresh chopped parsley
    Paprika

Brown and cook hamburgers in salad oil. Remove hamburgers to hot serving platter. Stir in mushroom soup, mushrooms, liquor, and sour cream. Heat through. Pour sauce over hamburgers. Sprinkle with paprika.

SWEDISH MEATBALLS

Ja . . . ja.

    MEATBALL MIXTURE
    ¾ C. cornflakes, crumbed
    1½ lb. ground beef
    2 eggs, beaten
    1½ tsp. salt
    ⅛ tsp. pepper
    ¼ tsp. nutmeg
    ¼ tsp. allspice
    ⅛ tsp. ground cloves
    1 C. milk
    3 tbsp. shortening or beef fat

GRAVY
3 tbsp. flour
1½ C. beef stock
¾ C. hot milk
½ tsp. salt
¼ tsp. pepper
½ tsp. MSG
2 tbsp. chopped fresh parsley

Mix all meatball ingredients together. Shape in 1-inch
balls. Brown in shortening or beef fat. Remove meatballs
to large pot. Blend in flour to shortening or fat. Gradually
add stock, milk, and seasonings while stirring. Pour over
meatballs. Cover and simmer 20 minutes. Before serving
sprinkle with parsley. *Serves 6.*

SWISS FONDUE BOURGUIGNONNE

For a cook-your-own party.

2 lb. lean beef tenderloin, cut in 1-inch cubes
Watercress or other greens
Salad oil to give 1½- to 2-inch depth in fondue pot

Mound beef cubes on bed of watercress or other greens
on individual china or wooden dinner plates. Pour salad
oil into saucepan and heat to the point that a bread cube
browns in 1 minute. Pour heated salad oil into fondue pot.
Place on stand and ignite fuel. Have guests use long-
handled forks to spear meat and cook in the hot oil. Each
may cook to his individual liking. Serve a variety of
sauces: Brown Sauce, *Sauce Tomate,* Hollandaise, *Sauce
Piquante.** Serves 4 to 6.*

* See *Index.*

VEAL BALLS

A ground meat variation.

1 lb. ground veal
½ lb. ground pork
¼ C. minced onion
2 tbsp. milk
1 egg
½ tsp. salt
½ C. bread crumbs

Combine all ingredients. Shape into balls. Place in well-greased baking pan. Brown in preheated oven (350°F.) for 15 to 20 minutes. Pour ½ cup beef stock into pan. Continue baking for 15 minutes. Remove balls. Make sauce out of stock and drippings. Variation: Add 1 can of undiluted mushroom soup for a quickie topper over the veal balls. *Serves 4 to 6.*

VEAL SHANKS

A touch of spirits for zest.

All-purpose flour
8 pieces veal shank, 4 inches long
¼ C. salad oil
1 tsp. salt

½ tsp. pepper
¼ C. chopped onion
1 clove garlic, cut in quarters
¼ C. all-purpose flour
2 C. brown stock
¼ C. white wine
¼ C. tomato purée
1 tsp. chopped fresh parsley
1 tsp. grated lemon rind

Flour the shanks and brown in oil. Remove to a 3-quart pot. Season with salt and pepper. Sauté onion and garlic in the same oil for 3 minutes. Add flour. When it thickens, add stock, stirring constantly. Add wine and tomato purée. Bring to boil. Pour over shanks and cover pot. Bake in preheated oven (350°F.) for 1½ hours. Remove shanks to hot platter. Add parsley and lemon rind to sauce. Simmer 5 minutes. Pour over shanks. *Serves 8.*

Dressings, Gravies, and Sauces

At the time Mama was young and raising her family she had not yet been to France, nor, by her admission, had she read a cookbook of gourmet cuisine. Yet there was that spirit of adventure and inquiry in her makeup that rejected the ordinary. She experimented with her recipes as a scientist might with his test tubes. She added pinches of spices, leaves of herbage; substituted ingredients that would add piquancy to an established flavor or a sweetness or a dash. From this desire to explore the new came her particular way with sauces and gravies. A leftover to my Mother was a challenge that came to be a family joke. "What do you call this, Mama?" we would tease. And to the hash or goulash of most homemakers she would have added a sauce that had simmered on the back burner most of the day and that she had compounded from many tastings from the wooden spoon. She used to rise to our banterings and say, "That is Red Witch Stew" or "Herbed Beef Basket." These names, as well as the results we delighted in, made them oft-repeated family standbys. Mama could remember to the half teaspoon the ingredients of the dishes we praised the most and could easily duplicate them.

I have been to France and have read the best of many a French chef in the original; but it is from these long-ago successes that many of the compliments come from our restaurant patrons. Often when we are particularly praised for a sauce, I can so easily hear echoing the words "What do you call this, Mama?"

BAKED HAM GLAZE

Brush it on.

½ C. light brown sugar, firmly packed
3 tbsp. cornstarch
½ C. honey
2 C. hot water

Combine all ingredients in saucepan. Cook over medium heat, stirring constantly until mixture is clear and transparent. Take ham from oven and brush on glaze. Let stand 15 to 20 minutes before carving.

BORDELAISE SAUCE

Made this way at Hôtel Georges Cinq.

½ C. red wine
2 shallots, chopped fine
½ tsp. freshly ground pepper
⅛ tsp. thyme
1 small bay leaf
3 C. brown sauce
2 tbsp. butter
¼ C. diced beef marrow

Simmer wine, shallots, pepper, thyme, and bay leaf for 8 minutes. Add brown sauce and simmer gently for 20 minutes. Add butter. Strain through cheesecloth. Poach beef marrow in boiling water for three minutes. Remove marrow with slotted spoon and add to sauce. Serve on your choice of steak.

BROWN SAUCE

Affectionately called "espagnole."

   ½ C. beef fat, melted
   2 C. chopped onion
   ½ C. chopped carrot
   ½ C. all-purpose flour
   2½ qt. brown stock
   3 sprigs parsley
   1 stalk celery
   ½ bay leaf
   ⅛ tsp. thyme
   ¼ C. tomato sauce
   Salt
   Pepper

Sauté onions and carrots in beef fat until onions are light brown in color. Stir in flour. Add 4 cups stock, stirring constantly. Add parsley, celery, bay leaf, thyme, and 4 cups stock. Simmer gently 1 hour. Strain through sieve. Add 2 cups stock and tomato sauce. Simmer 1 hour. Cool and refrigerate. Peel off fat. Reheat when ready to use and season with salt and pepper. *Makes about 3 quarts.*

CHEESE SAUCE

A big topper for vegetables or fish.

1 recipe medium white sauce*
1 C. shredded cheddar cheese
½ tsp. dry mustard

Combine all ingredients in saucepan over low heat. Stir constantly until cheese melts and sauce is smooth. *Makes approximately 3 cups.*

CHICKEN MARINADE

The inelegant chicken becomes *poulet.*

5 tbsp. salt
2 tsp. MSG
1 gal. water

Mix all together. Pour over chicken. Refrigerate 4 hours or overnight. Remove chicken and pat dry. Chicken is ready to be made up (i.e. fry, bake, or broil).

COCKTAIL SAUCE FOR SEAFOOD

Just tangy enough.

2 C. catsup
2 tsp. horseradish
2 tbsp. lemon juice
2 tbsp. sugar
Dash tabasco sauce

* See *Index.*

½ tsp. celery salt
½ tsp. salt
½ tsp. pepper
2 tsp. Worcestershire sauce
½ C. chili sauce

Mix all together until well blended. Store in jar. *Makes 2¾ cups.* Variation: Use half cocktail sauce and half mayonnaise for a lighter and mellower sauce for fish.

COUNTRY INN BARBEQUE DRESSING

A basting for backyard barbecue get-togethers.

1 C. vinegar
1¾ C. tomato purée
3½ C. chili sauce
1½ tbsp. salt
½ C. sugar
3 garlic cloves, chopped
2¾ C. salad oil
1 tbsp. dry mustard
½ tsp. red pepper
2 tsp. paprika

Combine all ingredients in saucepan. Simmer 15 minutes. *Makes approximately 8 cups.*

EASY BARBECUE SAUCE

For ribs or chicken.

¼ C. butter
2 onions, finely chopped
3 tbsp. Worcestershire sauce
3 tbsp. steak sauce

⅓ C. brown sugar
½ C. lemon juice
¼ tsp. hot sauce
¼ tsp. celery salt
⅔ C. vinegar
2 C. catsup
2 C. water

Melt butter in skillet. Add onion and cook until tender. Add remaining ingredients and simmer 20 minutes. *Makes 5 cups.*

FAIL-PROOF HOLLANDAISE

A proven medal winner.

6 egg yolks
1 tbsp. lemon juice
¼ tsp. water
Dash of tabasco
¼ tsp. Worcestershire sauce
¼ C. bubbling-hot butter

Place egg yolks in blender. Add lemon juice, water and tabasco and Worcestershire sauces. Turn blender on low for 1 minute. Turn blender to high speed. Slowly add butter. Blend until thick and fluffy. Use over fish, broccoli, or asparagus. *Makes ½ cup.*

GOLDENROD SAUCE

A dinner sauce to accent or extend an entrée.

    1 C. medium white sauce
    1 tbsp. chopped fresh parsley
    2 hard-cooked eggs, chopped
    1 tsp. lemon juice

Heat white sauce until hot. Remove from heat. Mix in eggs, parsley, and lemon juice. Use over fish or chicken croquettes. *Makes approximately 1 cup.*

HORSERADISH SAUCE

Goes well with prime ribs or to glorify a more modest cut.

    1 C. heavy cream, whipped
    1 tsp. Worcestershire sauce
    ½ tsp. dry mustard
    2 tbsp. grated horseradish, strained

Mix all ingredients. Keep under refrigeration. *Makes 1 cup.*

ITALIAN SPAGHETTI SAUCE

With variations from *Firenze, Bologna, Sorrento*, and *Roma*.

    ½ C. salad oil
    1 C. chopped onion
    2 cloves garlic, minced
    ½ C. celery
    ¼ C. green pepper, diced
    2 qt. Italian tomatoes, crushed

1 C. beef stock
1 qt. tomato purée
½ tsp. sweet basil leaves
1 tsp. oregano
1 bay leaf
1½ tsp. salt
⅛ tsp. pepper
1 tsp. sugar
2 tbsp. chopped parsley
⅛ tsp. tabasco sauce

Sauté in oil the onion, garlic, celery, and green pepper for 5 minutes. Add remaining ingredients. Simmer 1 hour covered, in sauce pot. Remove cover and simmer ½ hour longer. Cool and refrigerate. Reheat the next day. *Makes about 3½ quarts.* Variations: (1) Add ½ cup canned mushrooms the last 15 minutes of cooking time. (2) Add ¼ cup Parmesan cheese with seasonings. (3) For meat sauce, add 5 cups lightly browned ground beef about ½ hour before sauce is done. (4) Add ½ cup sliced ripe olives at end of cooking time. (5) Add ¼ cup Burgundy wine the last 15 minutes of cooking time.

MILD TOMATO SAUCE

For your next meat loaf.

  2 tbsp. salad oil
  ¼ C. chopped onion
  ¼ C. chopped green pepper
  ¼ C. chopped celery
  2 tbsp. cornstarch
  2 tbsp. water
  1½ C. tomato purée
  3 C. tomato juice
  1 tsp. lemon juice

½ tsp. sugar
Dash of cayenne
1 tsp. salt
1 tsp. Worcestershire sauce

Sauté onion, green pepper, and celery in salad oil until tender. Dissolve cornstarch in water. Add to vegetables with the remaining ingredients. Bring to boil and then lower heat. Simmer 45 minutes. *Makes 1 quart.*

NEW ENGLAND CRANBERRY SAUCE

The gobbler is trussed as the family turns into the lane.

2 C. water
2 C. sugar
4 C. cranberries

Boil water and sugar 5 minutes. Add cranberries. Simmer until all skins pop, about 5 minutes. Do not stir. Cool. *Makes 4 cups.*

JELLIED CRANBERRY MOLD

Same as New England Cranberry Sauce, except boil sauce 15 minutes. Pour into 1-quart mold. Chill.

ORANGE GLAZE

Elegant buffet ham topping.

1 ready-to-eat whole ham
2 tbsp. unflavored gelatin
1½ C. strained orange juice

Dissolve gelatin in ½ cup orange juice. Heat over hot water until melted. Add 1 cup orange juice to gelatin mixture. Decorate ham with orange slices and maraschino cherries. Spoon mixture over ham and decorations. Refrigerate.

ORANGE RUM SAUCE

For roast duck supreme.

1½ C. orange sections
¼ C. cornstarch
2½ C. orange juice
2 tbsp. lemon juice
3 tbsp. sugar
½ tsp. salt
¼ C. light rum

Cut orange sections into ½-inch pieces. Dissolve cornstarch in orange and lemon juices. Bring to a boil. Add sugar and salt. Continue cooking until glossy. Add orange sections. Remove from heat. Cool. Add rum and stir. *Makes approximately 4½ cups.*

RAISIN SAUCE

For baked ham slices.

½ C. brown sugar
3 tbsp. cornstarch
¼ tsp. salt
2 C. apple juice
½ C. seedless raisins
⅛ tsp. ground cloves
⅛ tsp. cinnamon

Mix all ingredients together. Simmer until glossy. *Makes 2½ cups.*

SAUCE PIQUANTE

For fondue dipping.

1 C. Hollandaise Sauce*
1 tbsp. Dijon-type prepared mustard
⅛ tsp. sugar

Blend together.

SAUCE TOMATE

Another fondue dip.

1 C. Hollandaise Sauce*
½ C. tomato purée
⅛ tsp. sugar

Blend together.

* See *Index.*

SHERRY MUSHROOM SAUCE

Dine with wine.

½ C. fresh, sliced mushrooms
2 tbsp. butter
1 tsp. shallots
⅓ C. dry sherry
1 C. Brown Sauce*
1 tsp. fresh, chopped parsley

Sauté mushrooms in butter until lightly browned. Add shallots and cook 1 minute. Add remaining ingredients and simmer 5 minutes. Serve over meat or poultry.

STEAK MARINADE

For flavor and tenderness.

1 C. salad oil
1 tsp. coarsely ground fresh pepper
1 tsp. MSG
½ tsp. salt
1 tsp. garlic powder

Combine all ingredients and pour into shallow pan. Place steaks in marinade and flip them over. Let stand in refrigerator until ready to use.

* See *Index.*

SUPREME SAUCE

A royal sauce for gourmets.

1½ C. medium thick chicken stock
2 tbsp. canned sliced mushrooms
1 C. velouté sauce
1 C. heavy cream
½ tsp. salt
Pinch cayenne

Add mushrooms and velouté sauce to chicken stock. Simmer. Reduce until 1 cup remains. Add cream, salt, and cayenne. Strain through colander. *Makes about 1 cup.*

SWEET-SOUR SAUCE

For ribs, chicken, or beef cubes.

1 C. crushed pineapple
½ C. sugar
½ C. chopped green pepper
⅓ C. chopped pimento
1 garlic clove, minced
½ C. vinegar
¼ C. water
2 tbsp. soy sauce

¼ tsp. tabasco sauce
2 tbsp. cornstarch
¼ C. cold water

Combine pineapple, sugar, green pepper, pimento, garlic, vinegar, ¼ C. water, soy sauce, and tabasco sauce. Heat until it simmers. Combine cornstarch and ¼ cup cold water. Add to above. Cook, stirring constantly until thick and clear, approximately 10 minutes. *Makes 4 servings of sauce.*

TARTAR SAUCE

Can be stored for weeks in the refrigerator.

2 C. salad dressing
3 tbsp. minced onion
⅛ tsp. cayenne pepper
¼ tsp. minced dry parsley
¼ tsp. celery seed
2 tsp. pickle relish
2 tbsp. chopped olives
2 tbsp. chopped sweet pickles
⅛ tsp. garlic salt
¼ tsp. white pepper
¼ tsp. salt

Mix all together. Store in jar. *Makes about 2¼ cups.*

VELOUTÉ SAUCE

Excellent for croquettes.

⅓ C. butter
⅓ C. sifted all-purpose flour
3 C. veal or chicken stock

½ tsp. salt
¼ tsp. white pepper
⅛ tsp. nutmeg

Melt butter in skillet over low heat. Blend in flour. Cook over low heat until mixed. Gradually add stock, stirring constantly until thick and smooth. Stir in salt, pepper, and nutmeg. *Makes 3½ cups.*

THIN WHITE SAUCE

2 tbsp. butter, melted
2 tbsp. flour
1 C. coffee cream
¼ tsp. white pepper
1 tsp. salt
1½ C. meat stock seasonings or vegetable liquor

MEDIUM WHITE SAUCE

2 tbsp. butter, melted
3 tbsp. flour
1 C. coffee cream
¼ tsp. white pepper
1 tsp. salt
1 C. meat stock seasonings or vegetable liquor

THICK WHITE SAUCE

¼ C. butter, melted
5 tbsp. flour
1 C. coffee cream
¼ tsp. white pepper
1 tsp. salt
1 C. meat stock seasonings or vegetable liquor

Add flour to butter in saucepan. Cook over low heat. Stir in cream, seasonings, and meat stock. Heat to boiling, stirring constantly, for 1 minute. *Makes 2 cups.*

RICH WHITE SAUCE

Over croquettes or fish.

1 C. medium white sauce
2 egg yolks, slightly beaten

Mix together and reheat. *Makes 1 cup.*

ZIPPY CHILI SAUCE

Serve over rump roast.

1 C. chili sauce
¼ C. wine vinegar
¼ C. water
2 tbsp. light brown sugar
2 tbsp. Worcestershire sauce
½ C. chopped onion
½ C. finely chopped celery

Combine all ingredients. Simmer until vegetables are tender. Serve over rump roast. *Makes approximately 2½ cups.*

GIBLET GRAVY

As traditional to the holidays as the yule log.

Poultry neck, gizzard, wings, liver, and heart
1 tsp. finely chopped onion
1 tsp. salt
⅛ tsp. pepper
3 tbsp. all-purpose flour
¼ C. cold water

Boil poultry pieces until tender. Pour off excess fat into pan in which bird was roasted. Add enough stock from the gizzard mixture to make 3 cups stock. Chop gizzard, liver, and heart and add to stock. Add onion, salt, and pepper. Combine flour and water. Add to stock. Boil 3 minutes, stirring constantly. *Makes 3 cups.*

GOLDEN CHICKEN GRAVY

A poultry gravy without the headliner.

2 tbsp. chicken base
1 qt. boiling water
¼ C. butter or margarine
½ C. sifted all-purpose flour
1 tsp. sherry
¼ C. sliced canned mushrooms
½ C. sliced cooked carrots
2 tsp. chopped parsley

Dissolve chicken base in boiling water. Melt butter in saucepan. Add flour. Stir in water and chicken base slowly. Cook 5 minutes. Add sherry, mushrooms, carrots, and parsley. *Makes 4 cups.*

PAN GRAVY

Said to be the bride's nemesis.

¼ C. beef fat
¼ C. flour
2¼ C. meat drippings and stock
Salt to taste
Pepper to taste

After roasting meat, put it on a heated platter. Add
enough stock to meat drippings to make 2¼ cups and
cook over direct heat, stirring constantly to dissolve the
brown bits that cling to the bottom of the pan. Melt beef
fat and stir in the flour. Add the hot drippings to the
stock. Stir until gravy is smooth. Salt and pepper to taste.
Caramel coloring* may be used for a deeper color gravy.
Variations: Substitute ¼ cup coffee cream, ¼ cup milk,
or 1 cup canned mushroom soup for part of the liquid.

Poultry and Eggs

CHICKEN CACCIATORE

Make twice as much sauce and use for spaghetti.

2½- to 3-lb. fryer, cut up
6 tbsp. olive oil
1 C. minced onion
¾ C. minced green pepper
4 garlic cloves, minced
4 C. canned tomatoes
1 C. tomato sauce
½ C. Chianti wine
3¾ tsp. salt
½ tsp. pepper
½ tsp. allspice
2 bay leaves
½ tsp. dried leaves of thyme
1 tbsp. chopped fresh parsley
1 tsp. oregano
1½ tsp. tapioca
Dash cayenne
½ C. canned mushrooms

Wash chicken and pat dry. Brown in olive oil in large skillet until light brown. Remove chicken and add onions, green pepper, and garlic. Cook until tender. Stir in remaining ingredients and add chicken. Cover and simmer 30 to 40 minutes. *Serves 6 to 8.*

CHICKEN GOURMET

You are a show-off.

4 chicken breasts, each cut in half
½ C. margarine
1 clove garlic, minced
1 tsp. salt
¼ tsp. chili powder
⅛ tsp. pepper
⅛ tsp. dry mustard
2 tbsp. flour
½ C. coffee cream
½ C. milk
1 tsp. fresh parsley, minced
2 tbsp. almonds, toasted and slivered

Melt margarine in frying pan. Blend in garlic, salt, chili powder, pepper, and dry mustard. Brown chicken breasts on both sides. Cover pan. Bake in preheated oven (350°F.) for 40 minutes or until tender. Place on heated platter. Add flour to pan juice and stir until thick. Slowly pour in cream and milk until it thickens. Add salt and pepper to taste. Spoon over chicken breasts. Sprinkle with parsley and almonds. *Serves 4.*

EGGS BENEDICT

A classic Sunday brunch.

2 English muffins, split
Butter
4 slices boiled ham or Canadian bacon
4 soft poached eggs
Paprika
1 recipe Hollandaise Sauce*

Toast muffin halves. Butter each and cover with ham or bacon slice. Top with poached egg. Pour Hollandaise Sauce over egg. Sprinkle with paprika. Serve at once. *Serves 2.*

EGG SALAD SANDWICH

And variations.

6 hard-cooked eggs, shelled and chopped
1½ tsp. Worcestershire sauce
¼ C. chopped celery
1½ tsp. salt
¼ C. mayonnaise

Mix all ingredients lightly. *Makes filling for 6 sandwiches.* Variations: Omit celery and use ¼ cup chopped cucumber, ⅓ cup chopped bacon, 2 tablespoons pimento, or ¼ cup chopped green pepper.

* See *Index.*

THE FRENCH SOUFFLÉ OMELET

Pretty as a picture.

    4 eggs, separated and at room temperature
    ½ tsp. salt
    ¼ tsp. white pepper
    ¼ tsp. cream of tartar
    ¼ C. water or coffee cream
    2 tbsp. margarine
    Jam or jelly
    Confectioners' sugar

Beat egg whites, salt, pepper, and cream of tartar until
stiff but not dry. Beat egg yolks and water 1 minute with
same beaters. Fold egg yolk mixture into whites. Melt 1
tablespoon margarine in a divided omelet pan, coating
sides with part of it. Pour half of the mixture into each
side, folding the batter with spatula as it is being divided.
Keep over low heat until sides are lightly browned, approximately 8 to 10 minutes. Bake in preheated oven
(375°F.) 6 to 8 minutes or until puffy and light colored.
Loosen sides and put half on a hot platter. Put dabs of
jam or jelly on top. Cover with second half of omelet.
Sprinkle with confectioners' sugar. Serve immediately.
Serves 4.

QUICHE AT THE FARMER'S DAUGHTER

Or Onion Pie at the Country Cousin.

    1 thinly rolled pastry shell (8 inch)
    2 tbsp. butter
    ⅓ C. finely chopped onion
    ⅓ C. chopped Swiss cheese
    6 slices bacon, fried and chopped

2 tbsp. freshly chopped parsley
1 tbsp. Parmesan cheese
4 eggs, beaten
1¼ C. coffee cream
¼ tsp. salt
¼ tsp. white pepper
1 tsp. MSG
Paprika

Bake pastry shell in preheated oven (400°F.) just until it is light in color, about 15 to 20 minutes. Sauté onion in butter until transparent. Mix all ingredients except paprika. Pour into pastry shell. Sprinkle with paprika. Bake on bottom rack of preheated oven (325°F.) for 25 to 30 minutes or until custard is set in center when tested with the tip of a knife. Cool 10 minutes and serve, or serve it at room temperature or reheated in a 350°F. oven for 15 minutes. *Serves 6 to 8.*

MARSALA BRAISED PHEASANT

A bull's-eye any time.

2 pheasants
2 tsp. salt
2 tbsp. lemon juice
⅓ C. butter
Pheasant livers
2 oranges
¼ C. lard
1 4-oz. can mushrooms and juice
3 tbsp. butter
12 small canned onions
3 tbsp. flour
¾ C. Marsala wine
1 C. chicken stock

½ tsp. white pepper
Sprig of fennel or ½ tsp. fennel seed
3 juniper berries, crushed

Rub insides of pheasants with salt and lemon juice. Rub
outsides of pheasants with butter. Cut liver into eighths.
Cut oranges into eighths. Stuff birds with livers and oranges. Skewer birds. Put lard in heavy skillet. Bring to high
heat. Add birds. Reduce heat. Brown and baste. Light oven
to 400°F. When birds are brown, place in covered dish.
Sauté mushrooms and onions in fat, reserving juice from
mushrooms. Remove mushrooms and onions, and add
flour, wine, and chicken stock. Stir until sauce is smooth.
Add juice from mushrooms, salt, pepper, onions, mushrooms, fennel, and juniper berries. Pour sauce over birds.
Cover. Bake in preheated oven (400°F.) for 45 minutes.
Serves 4.

ROAST SQUAB

A succulent game dinner.

SQUABS
2 tbsp. fresh, chopped parsley
½ bay leaf
½ C. thinly sliced carrots
2 garlic cloves, minced
3 C. boiling water
3 tbsp. beef bouillon
3 squabs

GRAVY
3 tbsp. butter
3 tbsp. flour
¼ C. dry sherry
½ C. sliced canned mushrooms

In a large skillet combine parsley, bay leaf, carrots, garlic, boiling water, and bouillon. Place squabs on top. Bake in preheated oven (375°F.) approximately 1½ hours. Baste every 15 minutes. When done, place birds on a hot platter. Remove bay leaf. Melt butter and stir in flour. Add juice and carrots from squabs. Stir constantly until boiling. Add dry sherry and mushrooms. Pour over squabs. *Serves 6.*

Stuffing

GRANDMA STUFFS A TURKEY

"This," she said, "should be a family affair, for all youngsters love the excitement of this busy kitchen experience, plus the chance to be the first one to snitch a fingerful of dressing."

Each of us has her special method of "working over the bird," but Grandma said her way gave the turkey a "royal look," and of course she never stuffed a bird until it was ready for the oven. She added, "Since dressing expands during cooking, I leave a little space for *him* to breathe."

Her first step was to fill the neck cavity with dressing and then to fasten the neck skin to the back of the turkey with a skewer. I have seen her use a sharp, galvanized nail for the same purpose, and it did a neat trick, too. Next she lightly stuffed the bird and pushed the tail into the body cavity under a band of skin, also tucking the legs under the same band. She folded the wings and tucked them under the turkey, holding them with skewers. And of course the turkey got a good brushing with cooking oil, which Grandma spoke of as "fat."

I preheat the oven to 325°F., place the turkey breast side up on a rack in a shallow pan lined with foil, and push a meat thermometer into the thickest part of the fowl, avoiding the bone. When it is two-thirds done, I cover it all with heavy foil and continue roasting at 180°F. or 185°F. If no thermometer is used, the turkey will be done when the thickest part of the drumstick feels soft when pressed. I always let the turkey stand at least fifteen to twenty minutes for firmer carving.

Grandma never went by degrees. Her touch, smell and taste were all she needed to tell her whether the bird was fit to be eaten. And Grandma, bless her heart, garnished the old champ with parsley and bits of lemon to avoid that "naked look," she said, with a twinkle in her eye.

COOKING GUIDE

Heavyweight champ	16–20 lb.	4 to 4½ hr.
Middleweight champ	12–16 lb.	3 to 4 hr.
Lightweight champ	8–12 lb.	3 hr.

COOKING WILD RICE

1 C. wild rice
3 C. water
1 tsp. beef base
1 tsp. chicken base
3 tbsp. butter

Put rice in saucepan with water. Add beef and chicken base, and place over medium heat. Cover pan until water starts to boil. Remove cover and simmer without stirring over low heat for approximately 25 minutes or until there is no more water left. Put into warm bowl with a dollop of butter. *Serves 6.* Variation: Add ½ cup slivered almonds before serving.

APPLE PAN DRESSING

To fill a goose or turkey.

1 tbsp. margarine
2 tbsp. chopped onion
1 qt. finely chopped apples
4 C. 4-day-old bread
Cold water to cover bread
1 egg, beaten
1 tsp. salt
½ tsp. nutmeg
⅛ tsp. pepper
⅛ tsp. paprika
2 tbsp. fresh, chopped parsley

Sauté onion in margarine until transparent. Add apples. Cover bread with cold water for 5 minutes. Press out water and add bread to apple mixture. Add remaining ingredients and mix well. Place dressing in a greased pan (8 x 8 x 2 inches). Bake in preheated oven (350°F.) for 30 minutes or until lightly browned on top, or stuff a 6- to 8-pound turkey.

FRESH BREAD CRUMB DRESSING

Fish or fowl.

1 lb. fresh bread, frozen (18 slices)
½ C. cold butter
¼ C. chopped onion
¼ C. chopped celery
1 tsp. salt
¼ tsp. white pepper
1 tsp. sage (if using for fowl)

Cut crust from bread. Grind with medium blade. Grind cold butter with medium blade. Toss with bread. Add onion, celery, salt, pepper, and sage. Mix all together. Put into greased pan (8 x 8 x 2 inches) and cover with foil; or stuff fish or fowl. Bake in preheated oven (350°F.) for 30 minutes. *Makes enough to stuff a 12-pound turkey.*

MOM'S STUFFING FOR FOWL

Bygone farm days.

    1-lb. loaf of day-old bread (18 slices)
    2 egg yolks, slightly beaten
    1 tbsp. salt
    1 tsp. pepper
    1½ tbsp. sage
    1½ C. finely minced onion
    2 egg whites
    1 tsp. baking powder

Preheat oven to 250°F. and put bread on cookie sheet. Toast until golden brown and thoroughly dried. Soak in cold water and squeeze dry. Add egg yolks, salt, pepper, sage, and onion. Beat egg whites with baking powder. Fold into dressing. Place stuffing in bird when ready to bake. *Will stuff an 8- to 10-pound turkey.*

OLD-FASHIONED BREAD STUFFING

To fill a twelve-pound turkey.

    3 qt. fresh bread crumbs
    ⅓ C. chicken fat
    1 C. finely chopped celery
    1 C. minced onion

4 tsp. salt
1 tsp. poultry seasoning
1 tsp. pepper
1 C. chicken stock

Sauté celery and onion in chicken fat until tender. Add
to bread crumbs. Mix in seasonings and stock. For dry
stuffing, add less chicken stock. Cool, and place stuffing
in bird just before roasting.

OYSTER DRESSING

A stuffing for your rainbow trout catch.

20 drained oysters
2 tbsp. butter
4 C. bread crumbs
1½ tsp. salt
1½ tsp. pepper
1 tbsp. chopped, fresh parsley

Rinse oysters in cold water. Sauté oysters in butter until
sides curl. Add bread crumbs, seasonings, and parsley.
Mix carefully so that oysters will not be broken. Cool in
refrigerator for 1 hour. Stuff fish, turkey, or chicken.
Makes 5 cups of dressing.

PRUNE, APPLE, AND CELERY DRESSING

A fruity poultry stuffing; also good with chops.

1 lb. loaf bread, crumbed (18 slices)
⅓ C. butter, melted
1 C. cooked prunes, cut in ½-inch pieces
½ C. celery, chopped

½ C. apple, peeled and chopped
1 tsp. salt
¼ tsp. pepper

Combine bread crumbs with melted butter. Add prunes, celery, apple, and seasonings. Toss together lightly. Put into greased pan (8 x 8 x 2 inches). Cover with foil. Bake in preheated oven (375°F.) for 30 to 40 minutes. *Makes enough to stuff a 12-pound turkey.*

RICE STUFFING

Especially for your fish catch.

¼ C. butter
¼ C. chopped celery
¼ C. chopped onion
4-oz. can button mushrooms
½ tsp. salt
¼ tsp. pepper
½ tsp. poultry seasoning
2 eggs, beaten
1 C. cooked wild rice

Sauté celery, onion, and mushrooms in butter. Add seasonings and eggs. Cook over medium heat until eggs are set. Add rice and mix well. *Stuffs a 4- to 6-pound fish.*

SAUSAGE APPLE STUFFING

For pork chop pockets, too.

½ C. sausage
½ C. chopped tart apples
1 tsp. chopped onion
¼ tsp. salt
¼ tsp. pepper
½ C. hot water
½ C. bread crumbs
½ C. cracker crumbs

Fry sausage and cut in ¼-inch pieces. Add remaining ingredients and mix well. *Stuffing for small chicken (2 to 3 pounds).*

Seafood

LOBSTER THERMIDOR

The seafood supreme with royal sauce.

LOBSTER AND SAUCE
2 tbsp. minced onion
1 shallot, minced
¼ C. chopped mushrooms
1 tbsp. butter
2 C. thick White Sauce*
1 egg yolk
¼ tsp. dried mustard
¼ C. sherry
Dash of cayenne
¼ tsp. MSG
¼ C. Parmesan cheese
¾ C. chicken broth or vegetable liquor
3 C. canned lobster, cut in chunks

TOPPING
3 tbsp. bread crumbs
1 tbsp. grated Parmesan cheese
½ tsp. paprika

Sauté onion, shallot, and mushrooms in butter for 3 minutes. Add warm White Sauce and egg yolk. Stir in remaining ingredients and heat to simmer. Serve over rice mounds or in lobster shells. Blend together the bread crumbs and 1 tablespoon cheese. Sprinkle bread crumb mixture and then the paprika over filling. Broil until brown. *Serves 4.*

MARINATED FILLETS

Piquante marinade for flavorful fish or steaks.

2 lb. fish fillets or steaks
⅓ C. white wine
⅓ C. salad oil
2 tbsp. tarragon vinegar
2 tbsp. lemon juice
1 bay leaf
2 tbsp. chopped fresh parsley
1 tsp. salt
¼ tsp. pepper
1 tsp. Worcestershire sauce

Place fish or steak in shallow pan. Combine all ingredients and pour over fish or steak. Cover and refrigerate 4 hours. Place under broiler. Broil 15 minutes or until fish flakes easily when tested with a fork. Baste occasionally with marinade. *Serves 6.*

* See *Index.*

PAELLA BARCELONESA

A bit of Spanish cookery.

⅓ C. olive oil
1 garlic clove, minced
1½ C. chopped onion
½ C. chopped green pepper
1 lb. shrimp, cleaned, with tails left on
½ doz. mussels, well scrubbed
1 C. bite-size cooked chicken
4 squid, cleaned
1 large ripe tomato
3 tbsp. olive oil
2 C. Valenciano long-grain rice
2 C. chicken broth
½ tsp. crushed saffron
1 C. chopped chorizo (garlic-flavored sausage) or ham
1 tbsp. sliced olives
¼ C. pimento strips

Sauté garlic in ⅓ cup olive oil in large skillet. Add
onion and green pepper. Cover and simmer 5 minutes.
Cover shrimp and mussels with cold water. Bring to boil.
Cook mussels 1 minute or until they open. Cook shrimp 3
minutes. Save water. Add shrimp, chicken, and chorizo to
skillet, and stir. Add squid, and cook until curly and white.
Skin the tomato, cut in two, take out seeds, and chop into
small bits. Add to skillet. Heat 3 tablespoons olive oil;
when hot, add rice. Fry 5 minutes. Add rice, saffron, and
salt to skillet. Add 3 cups mussel liquor or enough water
to make it up; add chicken broth. Bring to boil. Simmer
on low heat until rice is done. Remove and place in large
paella pan. Decorate with mussels, pimento, and sliced
olives. *Serves 10.*

RED SNAPPER

Succulent ocean fare; tempting to the fish fancier and others.

6 8-oz. snapper fillets
¼ C. water
¼ C. butter, melted
1 tsp. lemon juice
½ tsp. salt
¼ tsp. pepper
Paprika
¼ C. toasted almonds

Skin fillets. Lay fillets in pan with water, butter, and lemon juice. Sprinkle with salt, pepper, and paprika. Put under broiler until brown. Bake in preheated oven (350°F.) for 10 minutes. Place on top of stove over medium flame for 1 minute. Serve on hot platter. Top with almonds and additional melted butter. *Serves 6.*

SOUTHERN FRIED CATFISH

Don't forget the hush puppies.

1 egg
2 tbsp. milk
¾ tsp. salt

⅛ tsp. pepper
1 C. flour
1 C. commercial dry bread crumbs
2 lb. catfish

Blend egg, milk, salt, and pepper. Combine flour and crumbs. Dip catfish in egg mixture and roll in flour mixture. Fry in deep fat (350°F.) for 5 to 8 minutes or until fish is golden brown. Drain on paper toweling. Serve with hush puppies and tartar sauce. *Serves 4.*

Sandwiches and Snacks

CANDIED ORANGE PEEL

Afternoon nibbling or decoration for a cake top.

    Peel of 3 oranges
    Water
    1 tsp. salt
    Granulated sugar
    Corn syrup

Cover peel with water. Add salt. Simmer 30 minutes. Drain thoroughly. Cover with cold water. Drain and repeat 3 times. Cut in ¼-inch strips with scissors. Add enough corn syrup to cover. Cook slowly until peel is translucent. Drain. Roll in granulated sugar. Dry on wire rack. Keep in cool, dry place. Use as cake decoration or for nibbling.

COCKTAIL SPREAD

For crackers or toast rounds.

⅓ C. canned mushrooms
1 tbsp. butter
1 package (8 oz.) cream cheese
1 tbsp. grated onion
¼ tsp. Worcestershire sauce
1 egg yolk
¼ tsp. salt

Sauté mushrooms in butter. Whip cream cheese. Beat in onions, Worcestershire sauce, egg yolk, mushrooms, and salt. Spread on crackers or rounds of bread on the untoasted side. Broil 3 minutes. *Makes about 1 cup of spread.*

FRENCH FRIED SANDWICHES

Or use as a French toast dip.

SANDWICHES
8 to 10 slices bread
Butter
Mayonnaise
Ham, tuna salad, or cheese
Sliced pickles

DIP
¼ C. eggs, whipped
¼ C. milk
½ C. cornflake crumbs

Spread butter and mayonnaise on each slice of bread. Fill with ham, tuna salad, or ham and cheese. Cut sandwiches in two. In a shallow dish add milk to eggs and blend together. Dip each sandwich in egg mixture; then in cornflake crumbs. Fry (375°F.) for 1 minute or until golden brown on both sides. Serve with sliced pickles.

OPEN-FACE SANDWICH

Broiled luncheon bubble.

4 slices bread, toasted on one side
Mayonnaise
4 slices American cheese
8 slices tomato
8 slices bacon, partially fried

Spread mayonnaise on untoasted side of bread slices. Place cheese on mayonnaise. Top with tomato slices. Crisscross bacon strips on tomato slices. Broil until cheese is bubbly. *Serves 2.*

POPCORN SNOWBALLS

For Hallowe'en tricksters.

3 qt. popped corn with all kernels removed
1 C. molasses
½ C. sugar
1 tbsp. butter
½ tsp. salt
Water or oil

Cook molasses, sugar, butter, and salt until mixture forms a very hard ball in cold water. Pour syrup over popped corn and stir. Dip hands in water or oil, and roll corn lightly into balls. Variation: If you want them extra special, add broken walnut meats just before shaping. *Makes about 14 balls.*

POPPY KOCK

Homemade, it has to be good.

   1½ qt. popped corn (⅓ C. unpopped)
   ¾ C. walnut halves
   ⅓ C. whole almonds
   1⅓ C. sugar
   ½ tsp. salt
   1 C. margarine
   ½ C. light corn syrup
   2 tsp. vanilla

Combine sugar, margarine, salt, and syrup in saucepan. Bring mixture to boil. Let simmer until it turns caramel color. Remove from heat. Add vanilla. Pour hot syrup over cookie sheet on which the popped corn and nuts have been spread. Mix to coat well. Cool. Break apart and store in airtight containers. *Makes 1½ quarts.*

SCAMPI

Chafing dish appetizer.

   3 garlic cloves, minced
   ⅔ C. butter, melted
   1½ tsp. salt

1½ lb. cooked shrimp, slashed lengthwise
⅛ tsp. ground black pepper
1 tsp. freshly chopped parsley
1 oz. dry vermouth

Mix all ingredients well. Cook 3 minutes. Keep hot in chafing dish.

SPREAD FOR SANDWICHES OR HOT HORS D'OEUVRES

Quick party snack.

8 oz. cream cheese
1 tbsp. grated onion
Dash of Worcestershire sauce
1 egg yolk
¼ C. chopped canned mushrooms

Mix all ingredients well. Spread on toast or cracker rounds and broil. Or toast one side of bread, butter the untoasted side and spread with mixture, and broil. *Makes 7 to 8 slices.*

SUGARED PECANS

Put in your silver compote for party nibbles.

1 egg white
1 tbsp. water
1 C. sugar
1 tsp. salt
1 tsp. cinnamon
1 lb. pecan halves

Beat egg white and water to froth. Mix well: sugar, salt, and cinnamon. Dip pecan halves in egg white mixture. Roll in sugar mixture. Place in shallow pan. Bake in pre-heated oven (300°F.) for approximately 30 minutes, stirring after 15 minutes.

SUMMER SHRIMP DIP

For the next patio cocktail party.

    1 C. canned shrimp, drained
    ⅔ C. commercial sour cream
    2 tsp. horseradish
    ¼ tsp. white pepper
    2 tbsp. French dressing
    1 tsp. Worcestershire sauce
    ½ tsp. salt

Put shrimp through medium grinder. Mix all ingredients together. Beat 3 minutes. Serve in bowl. Dip as you like with crackers, chips, or vegetable slims. *Makes approximately 1½ cups.*

Pickling and Canning

On our farm we had two big blue granite pans, and when Mother canned they covered the top of the black iron range that had belonged to Aunt Sarah, which Mother inherited.

In the spring we would gather sap and boil down a small amount in the pan to hurry up the process of maple syrup for our table. Winters we packed the pan full of snow and poured the hot syrup on top for chewy wax— that was our version of the city kids' penny candy. Through fall into spring Mother made big batches of applesauce and cottage cheese, and when not on the stove these pans were the storage space for the mountains of cookies we put away for Christmas gift giving. But at summer's end the real purpose of these pans came into play: fruits, vegetables, jams, preserves, all had their day. The pungent odor of hot spices or the fragrance of fresh fruit permeated the house, the yard, and beyond. All of the Nortons old enough to read had sugar to measure and spice bags to assemble. All of the Nortons old enough to be careful with a knife had cutting and peeling chores to do. This was "togetherness" before it became a magazine fad. We all felt we were part of our winter provisions, and we all knew this was the economy that made bicycles and doll carriages and patent leather Mary Janes a possibility. Papa called these sessions his "factory-worker-lunch days" because he would stay in the fields at noon and eat fruit and vacuum bottle coffee he had carried with him in the morning. Although by sundown there were finished rows of newly canned jars cooling in the pantry, the next day's work was half begun with a fresh supply soaking or marinating. These were the times we would supper with cheese and a salad down by the brook.

Modern kitchens would have no use for these blue granite pans, and probably no closet is big enough to store them. They went out of vogue just long enough to become a rarity. One day when I was browsing in an antique shop downstate, there on a table, displayed like choice china, were several pieces of blue granite ware: a kettle, coffee pot, and a big dishpan. I was not surprised when the dealer said the pieces were priced high since they were hard to find. As I looked at them—chipped, well used, and hauntingly familiar—I wondered what had become of the ones Mother was still using when we left the farm. I could smell pickling spices, see steaming pots, hear the bustle and movement of a canning kitchen; and there was a reluctance to leave the spot of blue that had brought me so sharply back to a childhood memory.

BAKED SWEET APPLES

Nutritious dessert.

Mother never worried about desserts when we had unexpected guests. She just brought up a jar or two of sweet apples from the cellar, whipped up some cream for a topping, and served it as a dish fit for any company. Mom always canned about 36 quarts for an emergency; and come fall, winter, spring, or summer, they were a favorite.

    Apples, washed and cored
    2 C. sugar
    3 C. water

Make a syrup of the water and sugar. Boil 5 minutes. Put apples in syrup and simmer until tender, being careful to keep apples whole when turning them. If syrup does not seem thick enough, remove apples and boil syrup a few moments longer, then replace apples and reheat. Lay fruit in jars and pour boiling syrup over. Seal at once. It is the heavy thickness of the syrup that makes this such a delicious dessert.

COLD BEAUTY PRESERVES

Bright and plump berries.

This recipe is so easy, you will do several pints and call it fun. So tidy up your kitchen, put on your prettiest apron, and get out a good size kettle and a wooden spoon.

    5 C. whole strawberries
    2 C. sugar
    1 lemon
    3 C. sugar

Wash and hull the berries. Place in kettle with 2 cups sugar. Bring to a boil, being careful not to crush the fruit. Add 3 cups sugar and the juice of 1 lemon. Boil for 18 minutes, moving mixture around gently with spoon. Remove from heat and let stand for 12 hours or overnight. Put cold jam in sterile glasses without reheating and seal. *Yields about 1 quart.* When fruit is stored overnight, the color is set and the berries keep pleasingly plump. Store in a cool, dark place.

CRYSTAL ORANGE PEEL

A candy, a garnish, and a cocktail strip.

I never think of candied orange peel as only a confection. Mother packed the sugared strips into glass jars for refreshing garnishes. A twist of peel is also good in an old-fashioned. If you have a flare for color, tint them red and green. And if you have a "mother's helper," this is a "grown up" item to start her canning career.

Peel from thick-skinned California oranges
1 C. sugar for each 2 C. peel
1 C. water for each 2 C. peel

Cut peel in narrow strips. Cover with cold water and set aside. Boil proper measure of sugar and water until thick and syrupy. When sugar spins a fine thread, add peel. Cook until peel is transparent. Spread on waxed paper. When peel begins to cool, roll the strips in granulated sugar. Store in covered jars.

FOUR-SEASON PICKLED FRUITS

For winter doldrums.

Did you ever get the canning fever in the winter, when icicles hang like glass fringe across your windows? Even in cold weather the urge to can can be satisfied if you will reach for some fruit and a can opener. So let's turn winter into summer, which is a delight for the imagination and morale.

    4 C. peach halves, drained
    1 C. water
    1 C. sugar
    1 C. vinegar
    2 sticks cinnamon
    2 tsp. whole cloves
    2 tsp. allspice
    1 tsp. mace

Combine water, sugar, vinegar, and all spices. Drop peaches into syrup and boil gently 15 minutes. Pack peaches in sterilized jars and cover with hot syrup and seal. *Makes about 2 pints.* Pickled fruit makes a more attractive garnish than just fruit from a can.

MANGO CHUTNEY

On the farm we made this in a big granite dishpan.

    1 lb. pitted and peeled mangoes, cut in small pieces
    1 pt. vinegar or ½ pt. grapefruit juice and ½ pt. vinegar
    ½ lb. currants
    ½ lb. raisins or 1 lb. raisins, if currants are omitted
    ¼ lb. blanched almonds

¾ lb. brown sugar
3 oz. sliced green ginger (may substitute broken pieces
    of root ginger and put in a bag)
1 tbsp. salt
½ tbsp. white mustard seed
½ C. chopped onion
½ C. chopped sweet peppers
1 oz. chilis or hot peppers

Bring vinegar and sugar to a boil. Add the remaining ingredients and boil for 30 minutes. Pack while at the boiling point in sterilized jars, and seal. Hint: Mangoes just beginning to color are the best selection.

ORANGE CRANBERRY RELISH

For any winter holiday.

1 orange
4 C. cranberries
2 C. sugar
½ C. dry sherry

Put whole orange with rind and cranberries through food chopper. Mix in sugar. Let stand at room temperature 2 hours. Add sherry. Refrigerate.

PICKLED DRIED APRICOTS

Another winter "pick me up."

You'll love them. They are appealing, too, and nice as a garnish when you want to pretty up a dish.

> 3 C. large dried apricots
> Water
> ½ C. sugar
> 3 tbsp. vinegar
> 18 whole cloves
> 2 sticks cinnamon
> ½ tsp. mustard seed

Wash apricots and cover with cold water. Boil gently 10 minutes. Add sugar, vinegar, and cheesecloth bag filled with spices. Bring again to boil and cook 15 minutes. Remove spices. Fill jars with apricots. Cover them with boiling syrup and seal hot. Since this recipe calls for dried apricots, you can pickle in any season. *Yields about 4 glasses of 4½ ounces each.*

PICKLED PEARS

A bounty crop deserves keeping.

Will one jar of pears stir a memory? Mother said yes. When she was a bride she shared Great Grandmother's farm home until her own was ready. It was late October, and Mother helped can pears in all styles and shapes. She peeled and cored, measured and weighed, baked, spiced, and preserved, until the last pickled pear, Grandma's favorite, went down into the cellar. When Mother moved, her one thought was, "I never want to see another pear again." When Grandma called soon after they were settled, she brought a dozen jars! Mother said that they were a mainstay for her first housekeeping winter and a lesson that she should never again begrudge a beautiful orchard.

2 qt. pears
2 C. vinegar
4 C. sugar
1 small package cinnamon sticks
1 tbsp. mustard seed
1 tsp. cloves
Red or green vegetable coloring*

Peel pears but leave on the stems. Steam until tender but not soft. Make a syrup of vinegar, sugar, and spices tied in a bag. Put steamed fruit in jars. Remove spice bag. Pour boiling syrup over the fruit. Seal at once. A drop or two of vegetable coloring may be added to the syrup to give color.

PRETTY PICKLED CRAB APPLES

For palate and eye appeal.

In my company cupboard I always keep a few extra jars to adorn hot or cold meat platters, and crab apples just love roast beef and baked ham. Each complements the other.

6 lb. crab apples
3 doz. whole cloves
4 2-inch sticks cinnamon
10 blades mace

* Optional.

6 C. vinegar
6 C. water
9 C. sugar

Wash crab apples. Remove blossom end, but leave on stems. Prick skins several times with a large needle. This helps apples to keep their shapes. In a cheesecloth bag put the cloves, cinnamon, and mace. Boil the spice bag with vinegar, water, and sugar for 5 minutes. Add apples and heat slowly to keep their bodies from bursting. Simmer just until tender. Remove spices and put crab apples in sterilized jars. Pour on syrup and seal hot. *Makes about 3 quarts.*

SUN-COOKED PEACH PRESERVES

While the peaches are getting their vitamin C, so can you.

Did you ever think of taking a sunbath with peaches? Then give it a try. It is a most delightful way of doing two things at once. Other small fruits can be preserved in the same way, but cherries should be pitted.

Peeled peaches
Sugar (1 lb. for each 3 lb. of fruit)
Water

Cut peaches in halves and remove stones. Place sugar in pan and add enough water to make a thin syrup. Simmer syrup over medium heat and add peaches. Cook 15 minutes, being careful to keep peach halves intact, reducing heat if necessary. Remove peach halves from syrup with loving care and place them one by one on platters or shallow pans. Boil down syrup until it is thick. Pour the hot syrup over the fruit. Put the peaches outdoors in the sunshine and cover with netting. Let them stand 2 or 3 days until mixture thickens and becomes jellied, but be sure to bring them in each night. When ready to can, pack in sterilized jars. Sprinkle sugar between each layer and seal with paraffin. This fruit may be dried in a very slow oven, but the outdoor method gives the cook a chance to bathe in the sun while keeping a close eye on the peaches.

AMBER MARMALADE

Pumpkin style.

Pumpkin, you say, is just for pies. If you are in doubt, this deserves a try. A small size pumpkin will do, say about 5 pounds.

  1 small pumpkin
  Sugar
  Lemon juice
  Ginger, crystallized*

Peel, seed, and cut pumpkin into chunks. To each pound of pumpkin add 1 pound sugar and ¼ cup lemon juice. Let stand overnight in a crock. The next morning, simmer slowly until pumpkin is tender and mixture sheets from the side of a spoon. Place in sterilized jars and seal as any jam. You may add crystallized ginger before cooking if you think it improves the flavor.

* Optional.

APPLE "SASS" BUTTER

Blossom fragrance remains in spread.

The fragrance of this delicious spread will stir your imagination until the first drop of jam meets your eye.

  1 gal. apple cider
  4 qt. apples, pared and quartered
  3 C. sugar
  1 tbsp. cinnamon
  ½ tsp. cloves
  ½ tsp. allspice

Cook cider down to half original volume. Add apples and simmer for several hours. Stir frequently. Add sugar and spices. Cook until thick, stirring frequently. Pour into hot, sterilized jars, and seal. *Makes about 6 pints.*

BERRY RED JAM

Helps make a pancake supper.

These three red fruits make this jam delightfully different, not only on warm biscuits and jelly rolls, but also on triple-decker country pancakes.

  4 C. red cherries, pitted
  4 C. red currants, stemmed
  4 C. red raspberries
  10 C. sugar

Bring berries and sugar to a boil and cook until the mixture reaches a thick jam consistency. Pour into hot, sterilized jelly glasses, and seal with paraffin. *Makes 12 small glasses.*

BLUE GRAPE CONSERVE

Down memory lane.

Once upon a time Great Grandmother's porch was sheltered by woody grapevines. They provided shade as well as fruit but offered temptation to porch sitters long before the grapes were fully ripe. Mother's last visit to Grandma's house was in the fall. As the two chatted and rocked, Grandma reached for a cluster of grapes, and as she handed them to Mother, she seemed to smile a good-bye. My imagination carries me back many years, and I'd like to make believe that this recipe was "born" in Grandma's kitchen, as it is a very old one.

    4 lb. blue grapes
    1 orange
    4 C. sugar
    1 C. seedless raisins
    ½ tsp. salt
    1 C. chopped walnuts

Wash grapes clean. Remove skins, but do not throw them away. Put pulp in kettle and boil 5 minutes. Put cooked pulp in sieve and rub it through to remove all seeds. Grind whole orange and put juice and all in with the grape pulp, sugar, raisins, and salt. Boil rapidly 10 minutes. Stir from bottom with paddle or a square pancake turner to keep mixture from burning and sticking, until it thickens as you like it. Add grape skins and boil 10 minutes longer. Remove from heat and stir in walnuts, mixing thoroughly. Pour into hot, sterilized glasses, and seal with paraffin.

CARROT MARMALADE

A better flavor than orange.

This vegetable and fruit mixture blends so beautifully together, for it is orange marmalade flavor at its best but without its bittersweet taste. It is a splendid way of utilizing carrots from your garden when oranges are at a premium. It can be made any time in any season, as carrots are no problem to find the year round. It is pretty in color, rich and golden, and is as delicious on toast as any jam.

    2 oranges
    2 lemons
    4 C. cooked carrots
    1 qt. carrot liquid
    6½ C. sugar

Remove seeds from oranges and lemons. Put fruit through grinder with carrots. Combine them with the carrot liquid and the sugar in a 5-quart saucepan. Cook slowly until thick, approximately 4 to 5 hours. Put in sterilized jelly glasses, and seal at once. *Makes 4 pints.*

DUCHESS JAM

Mother's first try.

Near Mother's childhood cupola-topped home, wild strawberries grew in abundance, and each morning she rose
early to pick the breakfast "dessert." But one day the
berries went into a kettle and not on the table. In honor
of her first try, the family called it Duchess Jam, after her
pet name. This is an easy recipe, but at mother's tender age
it was a big beginning. From this experience, canning became a prideful accomplishment.

    4 C. strawberries
    2 C. sugar
    Juice of 1 lemon
    3 C. sugar

Wash and hull the berries. Put in kettle with 2 cups
sugar. Bring to a boil. Add 3 cups sugar and lemon juice.
Boil 18 minutes. Let stand overnight covered. Put cold
jam in jars.

GRANDMA'S CROCKED JAM

Keep adding during the summer.

The big earthen jar stood fresh and clean in the pantry
with the ear handles on each side, waiting for the first
summer fruit. As a whiff of brandy pervaded the air,
Mother said to me in her joking way, "Grandma's crock."
We could hardly wait to start this delicious jam, and the
first fruits of the season would be the first in the crock
and the first to "taste" the brandy in the bottom of the
crock. This is one of the tastiest jams that ever went into

a jar or crock, and the easiest method of preserving small fruits, such as strawberries, raspberries, cherries, currants, and gooseberries. Peaches may be added, too.

Put 1 pint brandy in crock. As fruit varieties become available, put 1 cup of washed, peeled, or hulled fruit and 1 cup sugar in the crock. Stir each day until 16 cups of fruit varieties have been added. Add more brandy if total of fruit additions is more than 4 quarts. Cover crock and stir occasionally. Serve as a very rich dessert or as a condiment with meats.

GRAPE JELLY FROM BOTTLED JUICE

Almost homemade.

2 C. grape juice
3 C. sugar
½ C. bottled Certo (jelling aid)
Melted paraffin

Mix juice and sugar in large saucepan. (If unsweetened juice is used, increase sugar by ½ cup.) Bring to a boil over hottest fire and at once add Certo, stirring constantly. Bring to a full rolling boil, and boil hard for 1 to 5 minutes, according to thickness desired; three minutes is sufficient for firm jelly. Remove from fire, skim, pour juice into glasses, and seal with paraffin at once. *Makes about 5 glasses of 6 fluid ounces each.*

GREENGAGE PLUM JAM

Be on the watch for this scarce variety.

These high-quality plums are greenish yellow and were imported from France about 1725. As a child I'd rather eat them from a tree than spoon them from a jar. Each time I pass a roadside stand, I look for this particular plum, but the other varieties seem more plentiful. The flavor of the greengage is unique and worth the search. You will enjoy its taste at any meal.

Firm, ripe plums
Sugar (1 C. for each 1 C. pulp)

Cut plums in small pieces and remove the stone, but do not peel. Put in kettle and cover with cold water. Bring to a boil. Simmer until plums are tender. Add sugar, and cook until mixture is thick. Pack in hot sterilized jelly glasses, and seal. These plums retain their best flavor if not more than 4 cups are cooked at a time.

PEACH AND CHERRY CONSERVE

Red and yellow, catch a fellow.

6 C. diced peaches
9 C. sugar
2 small jars maraschino cherries, chopped
1 bottle Certo (jelling aid)

Boil sugar, peaches, and cherries with juice 30 minutes. Remove from heat and add Certo. Boil again 2 minutes longer, stirring constantly. Put into jars at once and seal with paraffin.

PEAR AMBER

For gift giving.

This conserve, put up in attractive jars with the recipe attached, makes a most unusual and delicious gift. Give it at Christmas or whenever an occasion calls for a sample of some special treat.

    4 lb. pears, peeled and cored
    1 no. 2 can crushed pineapple (2¼ C.)
    2 oranges
    ½ C. fresh lemon juice
    4 lb. sugar
    1 jar (4 oz.) maraschino cherries, chopped

Chop prepared pears. Chop and grind oranges. Add pineapple, oranges, lemon juice, and sugar to pears, and cook until thick. Add cherries, and cook 10 minutes more. While hot, pack in sterilized jars and seal. *Makes about 12 small jars.* You'll have a hard time keeping one for yourself.

PIEPLANT CONSERVE

A rhubarb sauce.

Don't let the name confuse you, for pieplant is nothing more than garden rhubarb. Years ago everyone had a patch in his garden, beside the barn, or by a fence. It was spoken of as a spring tonic good for all stomach ailments. Grandma tended her rhubarb with the same loving care as she gave her choice flowers. Mother grew it, too, when we lived in the country. Today we seldom taste it as sauce, but more often in pies and jams. Try Mother's old recipe, as it is so easy to do.

2 oranges
1 lemon
6 C. pieplant, chopped
6 C. sugar
2 C. seedless raisins
2 C. walnut pieces

Chop oranges and lemon; use juice and all. Add pieplant, sugar, and raisins. Mix well and let stand several hours. Cook over low heat until mixture thickens. Remove from heat and add walnut pieces. Cook 5 minutes longer. Fill hot jelly glasses and seal with paraffin.

TOMATO CONSERVE DELIGHT

Buy big during summer.

Tomatoes are never so expensive that one can't use them freely in canning and preserving. They are fun to grow, and often when one has no working garden, we find these plants used as a background in flower beds, or a few tucked here and there to fill an empty spot. This conserve can be made from canned tomatoes, but in the early fall, when we see them in the markets or on fruit stands, we usually have the desire to "can big," and we pick up all we need. Conserve differs from preserves and jams in that it is a combination of fruits, sugar, and nuts. But in this recipe I omitted the nuts and substituted raisins, which in my opinion go hand in hand with tomatoes. Conserves are not as thick as jams and are often used to garnish desserts, but you will find many excuses to use this delicious sweet.

1 lb. raisins
1 pt. water
3½ lb. ripe tomatoes, peeled
3 lb. sugar
1 lemon, chopped

Soak raisins in water for 1 hour. Cook tomatoes until soft. Put through colander. Cook tomatoes, sugar, lemon, and raisins until thick. Can hot and seal. *Makes about 6 pints.*

WILD PLUM JELLY

Best in small quantities.

Don't let the name keep you from making this delicious jelly, for any plums will do.

Underripe, tart plums
Water
Sugar (1 C. for each 1 C. juice)

Wash and remove stems from plums. Put in open kettle with just enough water to cover fruit. Simmer until skins split or plums are very soft. Put both plums and juice in a heavy cloth bag and drip overnight. Never squeeze the bag, or the juice will be cloudy. Boil juice 5 minutes, and then add proper amount of sugar. Boil again until syrup sheets from spoon. Skim when necessary. Pour into clean, sterilized jars. Make just a small amount at a time. *One quart of juice makes 4 to 6 glasses of jelly.*

DILLY BEANS

Did you know there are 4,280 beans to a bushel?

1 gal. water
1 gal. cider vinegar
2 C. salt
½ C. pickling spices
8 C. sugar

Mix above ingredients and place over heat until boiling.

¼ bu. green beans
For each jar:
¼ tsp. alum
1 clove garlic, cut
12 jars (qt. size)
1 tsp. dill or 2 dried dill heads

Wash beans and pack in jars. To each jar add alum, dill, and garlic. Pour boiling vinegar mixture over beans, and seal jars. Delicious served with martinis.

DRIED CORN

And how to serve.

Great Grandma never opened a can of corn; I doubt if ever she had any use for a can opener! "Every vegetable from my garden," she would boast, "is either on the vine or in my cellar." It would be a rare occasion to see this item on her shopping list, for corn was a vegetable she dried with loving care. Mother took many canning lessons from this proud old lady, and treasured them all.

There are two ways to dry corn: in the sun or in the

oven. Mother liked the oven method best. Only young and tender just-picked corn should be used. Cook ears in boiling water 2 to 5 minutes to set the milk. Cut kernels from cob and spread thinly on shallow pans lined with cheesecloth. Place in oven 3 to 4 hours at 150°F. Leave oven door open a few inches.

You can also cut corn from cob without cooking, and place directly in 150°F. oven on pans lined with cheesecloth or absorbent paper, and dry slowly for 2 days, stirring occasionally. Put dried corn in cloth sacks. Mom used sugar sacks, something you do not see today and may never see again. Fill sacks half full, put in a warm place for 3 or 4 days, and shake now and then. To store, put in glass jars in a dry place.

When ready to serve, soak corn overnight in cold water. In the morning simmer, using 2 cups of water to 1 cup of corn. When corn is tender, drain off water and add cream and seasoning.

GREEN TOMATO PICKLED SLICES

Strip your plants just before frost.

You'll be tempted to use these pickles before they are cured, for the aroma of mixed spices whets the appetite.

1 peck unpeeled green tomatoes, sliced
3 large peeled onions, sliced
1 C. salt, noniodized
Water
Vinegar
½ tbsp. dry mustard
½ tbsp. cloves
½ tbsp. ginger

½ tbsp. cinnamon
1 qt. vinegar
2 lb. brown sugar

Sprinkle salt through tomatoes and onions. Let stand overnight in crock. Drain thoroughly and scald in weak vinegar solution made of 1 part vinegar to 3 parts water. Drain again. Make a cheesecloth bag of all spices. Add to vinegar and brown sugar mixture. Put in tomatoes and onions and bring to a full boil. Boil for 15 minutes. Can in hot sterilized jars. Cool 24 hours before storing.

MOCK MINCEMEAT

Pies or plum pudding.

Old-timers often made this meatless mincemeat by "guess and by gosh," and this means by taste. Before the frost is on the pumpkin, you can pick your green tomatoes and start your fall canning.

4 qt. green tomatoes, chopped fine
1 C. cider vinegar
3 C. raisins
3 green apples
2 C. light brown sugar, packed
1 tsp. salt
1 tsp. cinnamon
1 tsp. cloves
1 tsp. allspice
1 tsp. nutmeg

Combine all ingredients in an 8-quart kettle. Bring to a boil and simmer 30 minutes. If you want to live it up, add some brandy just before the end of the cooking time.

It not only adds flavor, but it smells magnificent. *Makes approximately 6 quarts.*

PICKLED CABBAGE

An old standby with pizzazz.

This can be used as a vegetable in place of sauerkraut. Green cabbage may be used, but some prefer red cabbage because of the thicker leaves and stronger flavor.

4 qt. cabbage
4 tsp. salt, noniodized
½ tsp. pepper
¼ C. mustard seed
1 C. sugar
2 qt. vinegar
¼ C. pickling spices

Wash cabbage, removing outer leaves. Quarter and slice thin or chip in bite sizes. Mix with salt and let stand 10 to 12 hours or overnight. Drain slightly and add pepper and mustard seed. Pack in sterilized jars. Mix sugar, vinegar, and pickling spices, and bring to a boil. Boil 5 minutes and pour immediately over cabbage. Seal, and let ripen a couple of weeks before using. This is superb with corned beef and gives a relish to ham, sausage, and cold cuts.

PICKLED STRING BEANS

Worth the four-week wait.

Either wax or green beans may be used, but wax beans
make a more appetizing pickle.

    4 qt. beans
    Cold water
    1 tbsp. salt, noniodized
    1 qt. water
    2 qt. vinegar
    1 C. sugar
    2 cloves garlic, peeled
    4 tbsp. mixed spices

Wash beans and remove strings and ends. Let stand 30
minutes in cold water. Drain. Cover with salt-water brine.
Boil for 20 minutes over medium heat until slightly tender.
Drain again. Add vinegar, sugar, garlic, and spice bag to
beans. Cook 10 minutes. Remove spices. Put beans in
sterilized jars and pour hot liquid over them. Seal at once.
Ready to use in 4 weeks. Use as hors d'oeuvre, a salad, or
as a sweet-sour vegetable.

TEENY-WEENY PICKLED BEETS

Toothpick canapé fare to dip in sour cream.

Red is so colorful to work with and so pretty in glass that
you will enjoy making and admiring these pickles.

    1 qt. tiny beets
    1 qt. vinegar
    1 to 2 C. sugar
    1 tsp. salt, noniodized

Wash beets. Boil with roots and 1 inch of top until tender. Peel. Boil together the vinegar, sugar, and salt for 5 minutes. Add beets and simmer until very hot. Can and seal. These will keep indefinitely. If you want the beets party sweet, use 2 cups of sugar.

ANTHONY K.'S CHILI SAUCE

A multipurpose sauce.

You can't call this by any other name, because from the start to finish it is a man's sauce. So make a man's size batch to begin with.

½ bu. ripe tomatoes, skinned and sliced
1 qt. vinegar
3½ C. sugar
½ box cinnamon (small size)
3 tbsp. salt, noniodized
3 red hot peppers, chopped or ground
2½ lb. onions, chopped or ground
12 sweet green peppers, chopped or ground
¼ box cloves (small size)

Skin tomatoes "alive" by dropping a few at a time in a bath of scalding water, followed by a cold shower. Slice into your largest kettle with all the remaining ingredients in it. Cook 4 hours or until thick. Seal hot. *Makes about 9 quarts.* Why not double the recipe and make 18 quarts? A little more time and effort will do it.

GOOSEBERRY CATSUP

Gooseberries, sugar, vinegar, spices.

The thought of gooseberries makes my mouth pucker, and on a bush I abhor these hairy little creatures. But put them in a pie or jam, and you'll treat them with some respect. Gooseberry catsup is an old-time favorite and is good as a savory sauce with roast, stews, or any meat. It makes tomato catsup seem prosaic.

   3 qt. ripe gooseberries
   2½ lb. sugar
   2 tsp. allspice
   2 tsp. ground cloves
   ½ tbsp. cinnamon
   2 C. cold vinegar

Remove the stems from the berries. Wash and scald well. Put through a fine sieve. Add remaining sugar and spices. Boil 15 minutes. Remove from heat and add vinegar without more cooking. Bottle at once before it cools.

TOMATO CATSUP

English born.

The name catsup is much older than Great Grandmother's wedding dress, and it probably goes back several decades beyond that. The oldest cookbooks carry it, so no doubt its origin can be traced back over a hundred years. This fine recipe was given to my mother by Mrs. John Babcock in Scio, New York. My compliments to a very lovely lady. It is an old family recipe, handed down from her New England ancestors.

Tomatoes to make 8 C. juice
1 qt. vinegar
2 C. brown sugar
2 tbsp. salt, noniodized
1½ tbsp. dry mustard
1 tbsp. cloves
1 tbsp. cinnamon
1 tbsp. ginger
1 tbsp. red pepper
1 tbsp. allspice

Wash and cut up tomatoes and cook until soft. Put through sieve or cloth until you have 8 cups of juice free from seeds. Add remaining ingredients, and simmer about 3 hours. Pour into sterilized jars or bottles and seal at once. You can make this catsup when tomatoes are out of season by substituting tomato purée, and the family may never know the difference. Since seasoning is a matter of taste, use what appeals to you and what you have on hand.

BREAD AND BUTTER PICKLES

Good enough for a bread-and-butter hostess gift.

Almost every cookbook boasts of bread and butter pickles. This is exactly what they are—a good snack anytime—and children love to fork them out of a jar to piece on. Grocers' shelves have many varieties of pickles, but I believe this is the most popular one, and doubly so if the pickles are made in your own kitchen.

4 qt. very fresh cucumbers, sliced
1 pt. onions, sliced
½ C. salt, noniodized
Water or ice cubes
2 lb. brown sugar
1 qt. vinegar
1 tbsp. mustard seed
1 tsp. celery seed
1 tsp. turmeric

Wash and slice cucumbers, but do not peel them. Add onions. Cover vegetables with salted ice water or cubes. Soak for 3 hours. In a kettle combine remaining ingredients. Bring to a boil and add drained vegetables. Heat to simmering point. Avoid boiling, for this makes them soft. Pack in sterilized jars and seal. *Makes about 4½ quarts.*

CANDIED CHUNK PICKLES

Sugar and spice and a sister so nice.

Each year my sister Dorothy sent me her pet recipe for pickles. This is my favorite.

PICKLES
50 dill-sized cucumbers
Salt water
Boiling water
Lump alum
1 horseradish root
Boiling water

SYRUP MIXTURE

5 qt. sugar
2 qt. cider vinegar
1 small box celery seed
1 small box stick cinnamon
½ box whole cloves

Put enough salt in water to float an egg. Add cucumbers and soak for 7 days, weighted down with a plate and heavy stone so cucumbers are completely under brine. Drain, and cover with boiling water. Let stand 24 hours. Drain and cut pickles in ½-inch slices. Cover with boiling water; add alum lump the size of a walnut, and horse-radish root. Let stand overnight. Make the following syrup: Cook sugar, vinegar, celery seed, cinnamon sticks, and whole cloves (keep cloves separate in a bag). Boil until syrupy. Pour this hot syrup over the pickles. Leave cloves in 24 hours, and then throw them away. Pour the same syrup, drained and reheated to boiling, over the pickles each day for 4 days. Bring pickles to boil in the syrup. Can immediately with hot syrup in sterilized jars. Seal at once.

CROCK PICKLES

Gather an apronful.

An old-fashioned crock is as much a part of our early heritage as the patchwork quilts and feather mattresses. And so are the pickles that go into it. Grandma found this way of canning so simple, for it took no special ingredients or skill. She could gather up an apronful of cucumbers at a time, and with no fuss or bother drop them into the crock. Reminiscing as I am, where are the poke bonnets like the one that Grandma wore in her garden to protect her face from the sun? Today garden hats take their places, but they are not nearly as quaint as the one that Grandma tied under her chin. So it seems that crocks and pickles, gardens and bonnets, all add up to old-fashioned memories and a recipe that may please you.

> Small green cucumbers
> Boiling water
> Brine mixture proportions:
>   1 gal. cold vinegar
>   1 C. sugar
>   1 C. salt, noniodized
>   2 tbsp. dry mustard
>   1 tsp. alum, powdered
>   1 C. horseradish, grated

MONA'S PICKLED EGGS

My city neighbor contributed this exciting old recipe.

> 3 dozen hard-cooked eggs, shelled
> 1¾ C. sliced beets with juice
> ½ C. sliced onion
> 4 bay leaves
> 6 whole cloves
> 1 C. brown sugar, packed
> ½ tsp. red food coloring
> White vinegar or sweet pickle juice

Place eggs in stone or other wide-mouth gallon jar. Add all other ingredients, and finish filling jar with white vinegar or pickle juice. Split eggs and use for appetizers.

RIPE CUCUMBER CURLS

The last on the vines.

Mother watched her vegetable garden grow very closely. When she picked all the green cucumbers she needed, she left the others on the vines to ripen, and nigh a one was wasted. They were all made up into ripe cucumber pickles. When I helped pick them, I never thought they were good looking as vegetables go, but in a jar dressed up they tasted yummy. We picked them late in the summer, when the vines were shriveled and would crunch under our feet. Then after Mother got them peeled and bathed in brine, I would snitch one now and then, just to get the salt taste. They are truly a fine pickle and not to be ignored.

PICKLES
Ripe cucumbers, peeled and sliced
2 qt. water
2 tbsp. salt, noniodized
Fresh water

SYRUP MIXTURE
4 C. sugar
4 C. vinegar
4 C. water
2 lemons, sliced thin
4 1-inch sticks cinnamon
2 tbsp. whole cloves
4 tsp. whole allspice

Wash, peel, and slice cucumbers not too thin. Soak overnight in a weak salt-and-water brine. Drain the next morning and cook 15 minutes in fresh water. Drain again. Make a syrup of sugar, vinegar, water, and lemons. Add spices in cheesecloth bag. Simmer cucumbers in syrup until clear and tender. Remove spice bag, and discard it. Pack pickles in sterilized jars. Continue boiling syrup until it is thick. Pour over pickles. Seal hot.

SACCHARINE PICKLES

No sugar, less calories.

For anyone who has to watch his intake of sugar, these pickles are excellent. When Mother ran out of sugar, she would hasten to put up these pickles, while the cucumbers were young on the vine.

Cucumbers
1 gal. vinegar
1 tbsp. saccharine powder
1 tbsp. alum
½ C. salt
½ tbsp. dry mustard, scant

Wash cucumbers and dry on towel. If too large, they may be split lengthwise. Pack in dry, clean jars, and fill to overflowing with uncooked syrup made with remaining ingredients. They will keep well in crocks and can be used in 2 weeks.

STORY BOOK PICKLES

From Grandmother's cellar.

Grandmother's cellar was a magic place many years ago, cool winter and summer. The huge marble slab tables, when touched, sent chills up my spine. Open fruit shelves lined the walls, and whenever I found my favorites, Grandma let me take them home. The one thing that fascinated me the most was the big dumbwaiter that carried food down from the dining room above. I had dozens of free rides down into this enchanted cellar, providing, of course, that Grandma was having tea in the parlor. One day when we were playing hide and seek, Mother came down to look for me. I was hiding in a big stone crock, and when I raised up to say "boo," she said in amazement, "Why, you are in Grandmother's pickle crock."

That evening she told me more. Mother said, "From the time that I was a little girl, and right through my high school years, the crock was never empty." Mother's pickles were favorites, and my school friends often walked me home to "fish" all the pickles they could eat from the crock. By supper time Mother never understood why we were not hungry. Today, in memory of Grandmother's pickle crock, here is the recipe:

    10 C. salt
    20 C. sugar
    10 C. dry mustard
    20 qt. vinegar
    10 qt. water
    Fresh cucumbers

Mix all brine ingredients and put in large crock. Add cucumbers to fill. If large ones are used, slice lengthwise.

Leave for a few weeks. If you wish to cut down on the brine for a smaller crock of pickles, a little arithmetic will do that. Add more cucumbers and brine as supply dwindles.

WATERMELON RIND PICKLES

The good part that most folks throw away.

Start making these appetizing and delicious pickles from your first melon, and you'll prepare several batches before they are out of season.

PICKLES
2 qt. white meat watermelon rind
2 qt. water
2 tbsp. salt, noniodized
Water
½ tsp. salt, noniodized
½ tsp. alum

SYRUP
10 C. water
1½ qt. vinegar
2 tbsp. whole allspice
10 2-inch sticks cinnamon
2 tbsp. whole cloves
1 lemon, sliced thin

Cut off the green and the pink parts of rind, and cut the white into strips 2 inches long and 1 inch wide. Soak about 2 hours in 2 quarts water and 2 tablespoons salt. Drain and then boil until tender in fresh water with ½ teaspoon salt and ½ teaspoon alum. Drain again, and chill in ice water. Make a syrup of sugar, water, vinegar, and spices tied in a cheeescloth bag. Boil ingredients 5 minutes. Add sliced lemon and the melon rinds. Boil again until syrup is fairly thick and the rinds transparent. Remove spices and pack rinds with syrup to overflowing in sterilized jars. Seal hot. *Makes 2 quarts*. Let stand 4 weeks before using.

CORN RELISH

Serve with baked meats or as a sandwich spread.

So often when I see a field of corn waving in a summer breeze, I think of Mother in canning season. She seldom used accurate measurements, but no matter how she put corn relish together, it was good. Later she did try to figure out her recipe. You can't go wrong if you make this as I heard it.

5 C. corn kernels, cooked
½ C. sweet red peppers, chopped
1 C. onions, chopped
1 tbsp. prepared mustard
1 tbsp. mustard seed
2 tbsp. celery seed
1 tsp. turmeric
1 C. brown sugar
2 C. vinegar
2 tsp. salt, noniodized

Cook corn in boiling salted water until tender. Cut off kernels with a sharp knife, do not scrape ears. Combine corn with all remaining ingredients. Mix well and simmer slowly for 35 minutes. Seal at once in hot jars. *Makes about 5 pints*. This relish is good as a sandwich snack with most any kind of bread.

COUNTRY BEET RELISH

Almost no cooking.

This delightfully red relish has a characteristic flavor, as do all relishes. They help to stimulate the appetite and to render food more palatable.

 1 qt. cooked, skinned, chopped beets
 1 qt. chopped cabbage
 1 tbsp. grated horseradish
 1 tsp. salt, noniodized
 1½ C. sugar
 ¼ tsp. red pepper
 Cold vinegar

Mix well: beets, cabbage, horseradish, salt, sugar, and pepper. Cover with vinegar in crock or glass jar. Cover and seal. Keeps well in a cool place. *Makes about 2 quarts.*

CRANBERRY DATE CHUTNEY

Preserved fruits (cranberries, dates, sugar, vinegar, salt, spices).

This is perfect with the holiday turkey and good at any feast. I always put this spicy fruit condiment in small glasses, for a little goes a long way. There are many kinds of chutney, such as apple, gooseberry, and plum. But this is my top favorite, for the fruits and spices blend in a perfect combination of rich goodness.

 1 lb. cranberries, chopped
 ¾ C. dates, pitted and quartered
 ½ C. water
 ½ C. sugar

¼ C. vinegar
¼ tsp. ginger
¼ tsp. cinnamon
⅛ tsp. allspice
⅛ tsp. cloves
⅛ tsp. salt
¾ C. raisins

Combine all ingredients except raisins and bring to a boil. Boil 5 minutes, stirring constantly. Add raisins and boil 5 minutes more. Stir carefully so as not to break fruit. Spoon into small glasses. Seal at once with paraffin.

EASY CUKE RELISH

For hamburger and hot dog dressing.

Homemade relish has a better flavor and is not so strong as the store kind. So get busy when the cukes are on the vines, and make yourself a big batch.

    20 large cucumbers, peeled and seeded
    2 large onions, peeled
    4 tbsp. salt, noniodized
    1 qt. white vinegar
    1 C. sugar

2 tsp. mustard seed
2 tsp. celery seed
1 hot pepper, chopped

Grind cucumber and onion. Add salt and let stand 1 hour. Drain thoroughly. Add remaining ingredients. Cook 20 minutes. Can and seal hot. So good with those hot dogs and hamburgers.

GARDEN CHOW CHOW

An end-of-summer potpourri.

I call this the last-of-the-garden yield, as Mother made chow at the end of canning season. If our garden didn't produce enough leftovers, the neighbors often contributed and we had a community can.

1 C. salt, noniodized
4 qt. water
1 qt. large cucumbers
1 qt. onions, sliced
1 qt. cauliflowerets
1 qt. green tomatoes, quartered
1 qt. peeled pearl onions
1 qt. small cucumbers
4 green peppers
Water
1 C. flour
1½ C. sugar
6 tbsp. mustard
1 tsp. powdered turmeric
1 pt. cold vinegar
2 pt. hot vinegar

Mix salt-and-water brine solution. Wash and prepare vegetables, and place in brine solution. Let stand 24 hours. Drain. Simmer vegetables in fresh water until barely tender. Drain again. Mix flour, sugar, mustard, and turmeric to a paste with cold vinegar. Stir in hot vinegar and cook until thick. Add vegetables and simmer 10 minutes. Pack in sterile jars and seal at once. The sauce from this pickle is wonderful in potato and vegetable salads. You can eat it the next day, but it is better to wait 3 weeks.

GREEN GARDEN RELISH

Outmatches any grocer's product.

What a shame that some of us don't have a garden, for often we lose our perspective by the time we rush to a fruit and vegetable stand. You'll like this recipe as the aroma of cooking spices tantalizes your appetite.

    2 qt. unpeeled green tomatoes, chopped fine
    3 large onions, chopped fine
    1 large green pepper, chopped fine
    2 tbsp. dry mustard
    1 tbsp. celery seed
    3 C. sugar
    ½ tsp. salt, noniodized
    1 C. water
    1 C. wine vinegar

Combine all ingredients in a 5-quart kettle. Cook 1 hour. Pour into sterilized jars. Allow to age at least 4 weeks before using. *Makes 4 pints.*

LAZY CUKE RELISH

Y'all come—and help.

I know you will go on a pickling spree when you see this recipe. It requires no cooking, and you have no excuse if the day is hot. Not only that, but the work is split up into two parts, to give you an overnight rest period. When you expect company, make a triple batch and let them help peel and grind. Of course they'll hint for some, but it's inexpensive and wonderful, and their labor is worth a handout.

    4 large onions
    4 peppers
    10 cucumbers, peeled and seeded
    ½ C. salt, noniodized
    1 C. horseradish
    1 C. sugar
    1 tsp. mustard seed
    1 tbsp. celery seed
    White vinegar

Grind onions, peppers, and cucumbers. Sprinkle with salt and let stand overnight. In the morning drain well. Add horseradish, sugar, mustard seed, and celery seed. Stir well and let stand 1 hour. Pack in jars, cover with vinegar, and seal.

PICKLED PEPPER HASH

In the crock.

In colonial Virginia, relishes and conserves, as well as pickles and jellies, were staple table delicacies. Today we depend on our food markets for the same things that

Grandma made from scratch. So why don't we go olden days now and then, especially in canning season. Pickled relishes add zest and variety to all meals and are pleasing to the eye.

1 C. seeded, chopped green pepper
⅔ C. seeded, chopped red pepper
3 C. chopped cabbage
1 C. chopped celery
2 tbsp. salt, noniodized
2 tbsp. mustard seed
2 tbsp. brown sugar
1½ C. vinegar

Mix peppers, cabbage, and celery with salt. Let stand overnight. Drain thoroughly. Mix the remaining ingredients, and bring to a boil. Put vegetables in a crock, and pour the hot vinegar mixture over the top. Cool, and then cover. Keep under brine at all times. If you wish a sweeter relish add more sugar. *This makes about 1½ quarts.*

BLACK MAGIC

Cocktail cherries.

These cherries would "bounce" if you used all whiskey, but to omit the bourbon would break their spirit.

1 pt. black cherries
¼ C. sugar
Bourbon
Cider vinegar
¾ tsp. allspice
3 to 4 whole cloves
¼-inch stick of cinnamon

Wash and dry large sweet cherries, but do not remove
stems or pits. Place in 1-quart-size apothecary jar with
sugar. Cover cherries with equal amounts of bourbon and
cider vinegar. If you like spicy cherries, add the spices.
Put top on jar and hide it in a dark place 3 to 4 weeks.
Stir once each day until sugar is dissolved.

DANDELION BLOSSOM WINE

Gather early in the morning.

Unless we are country born, we may see no earthly
good in dandelion blossoms, that sweep a blanket of bril-
liance over fields and lawns. It is true that they are both
a weed and a pestilence, but they do offer us wine for a
little trouble and effort. Even in colonial days, it is said
that children were kept busy gathering the blossoms in
early summer as people made wine by the barrel.

Pick dandelion blossoms early in the morning, and be
careful not to have a particle of the bitter stem attached.

1 gal. dandelion blossoms
1 gal. boiling water
3 lb. sugar
1 yeast cake
¼ C. water
3 oranges, cut in small pieces
3 lemons, cut in small pieces
½ lb. raisins*

Pour boiling water over the dandelion blossoms. Let stand 3 days. Strain. Add sugar, yeast which has been softened in water, oranges, lemons, and raisins (if desired) to the liquid. Let stand 3 weeks to ferment. Strain, bottle, and seal. *Makes about 6 pints.*

*Optional.

DELUXE EGGNOG

Can be used for a sauce.

  6 eggs, separated
  ⅔ C. sugar
  1 qt. coffee cream
  1 pt. heavy cream, whipped

Leave eggs at room temperature for 1 hour. Beat whites until fluffy. Add ⅓ cup sugar, and continue beating until stiff but not dry. Beat yolks and ⅓ cup sugar until light and lemon colored. Stir into the separated yolks and whites 1 pint of coffee cream each. Fold whipped cream into yolks. Combine yolks and whites together until mixed well. Refrigerate until ready to use. *Makes 1½ quarts.*

GREEN GARLIC OLIVES

Dry martini conversation piece.

  2 C. drained green olives
  2 garlic cloves, minced
  2¼ C. olive oil

Place all ingredients in 1-quart jar. Store in refrigerator for 3 days before using. Serve in salads or as an accompaniment to drinks.

HARVEST WINE

From the cellar of Duke Manor.

"Duke Manor" became my parent's home when I was in my teens. It was on Chautauqua Lake, and although this resort was known primarily as a summer colony, a few families lived there the year around; we were one of them. Point Chautauqua is in the heart of the grape country, and here I watched grapes grow up from vine to fruit. Mother smothered herself with this fruit when it was in season. Her jams and jellies lined our cellar shelves in abundance, and so did our harvest of wines.

9 lb. blue grapes
¾ lb. sugar
Cold water

Wash grapes and add sugar. Put both in an 8-quart crock, and fill with cold water. Cover with cheesecloth and keep in a warm place. Stir twice a week for 6 weeks. Strain and let juice stand 2 weeks longer to settle. This time do not stir. Bottle and cap. Try making a small amount at first, and then go big! For your second try, get ½ bushel of grapes. This is simple to make and easy to bottle.

HAYMAKER'S BEER

Field hands' refreshment break.

When my mother was young, Grandpa Dexter bought a farm which the family used for vacations in the summer. As a child, Mother carried this thirst-quenching drink to the workers in the fields, because as Grandma put it, "It helps to thin their blood." This seasoned water with ginger flavor was refreshing and made a good substitute for ice water, which most country homes were without.

1 gal. water
2 C. sugar
1 C. molasses
1 C. vinegar
1 to 2 tsp. ginger

Mix all ingredients and keep cold. This "poor man's beer" would not likely be served for a New Year's toast, but in the hayfield it was every man's drink.

MANHATTAN CHERRY

Versatile brandied berries.

Does this sound expensive? It all depends upon the way you use them. For snacking, yes; but for some special occasion, no. Be sure you keep from nibbling, as the "bite" is delicious.

3 qt. red cherries
1 C. sugar
Brandy

Wash cherries, but do not remove stems or pits. Pack in pint jars in alternate layers with sugar. Leave 1 inch space at top, fill jars with brandy, and seal. Let stand 28 days. The first week only, turn the jars upside down each day, so that the sugar and brandy will mix. *Makes about 6 pints.*

RASPBERRY VINEGAR

A refreshing drink. This is good, and simple to make.

Equal amounts of:
Raspberries
Vinegar
Sugar (5 lb. for each 3 qt. of juice)

In a crock combine equal amounts of berries and vinegar. Let stand 8 days, stirring each day. Mash and strain juice through cheesecloth. For every 3 quarts of juice, add 5 pounds of sugar. Boil 8 minutes and skim. When cool, bottle and seal. Put ⅛ cup of raspberry juice in a glass and fill with carbonated soda.

SANGRÍA

A cooler for warm summer months.

1 bottle (fifth) good dry red wine
1 pt. club soda
¼ C. lemon juice
¼ C. orange juice
1 oz. cognac
4 slices of lemon
4 slices of orange
¼ C. simple syrup*
2 cinnamon sticks
8 ice cubes

Mix all together. Pour into clear glass pitcher. *Serves 6 to 8.*

* See *Index.*

TOM AND JERRY

The perfect drink for an old-fashioned English country Christmas.

Deluxe Eggnog*
⅓ C. water
⅓ C. brandy
⅓ C. rum
Nutmeg
4 cinnamon sticks

Take hot mugs and fill ⅓ full with Eggnog. Heat water, brandy, and rum to boiling point. Divide into cups. Sprinkle with nutmeg. Put in cinnamon sticks. *Serves 4.*

CRYSTALLIZED ROSEBUDS

Use for decorations or for preserves.

Back as far as the thirteenth century, I am told, flowers were preserved in sugar and honey, and the sweeter the flower, the tastier the product. I well remember the mass of wild pink roses that splattered the picket fence on Great Grandfather Norton's farm.

Great Grandma Norton made these delicate preserves, and she preferred the pink roses and their light fragrance to all others. She gathered the roses in the morning and always picked the choicest buds. I have wondered many times if this was the recipe she used, but you will love to make them for their beauty and flavor.

* See *Index.*

4 C. tiny rose buds
2 C. sugar
1 C. hot water

Wash and stem rosebuds. Carefully shake dry. Dissolve sugar in water. Add the buds. Cook over medium heat until the syrup reaches the soft-ball stage when a small amount is dropped into cold water. Always stir gently. Remove from heat and continue stirring until the syrup reaches the texture of coarse meal. Put in a colander and shake off the excess sugar. Cool, put roses in jars, and seal.

DUTCH CHEESE

We call it cottage cheese today.

Mother always called it Dutch cheese, so I gather this is an old name; today we speak of it as cottage cheese. On the farm we were never without it. Our family cows produced more milk than we could consume, so our neighbors and friends shared with us. It takes a lot of sour milk to make a little cheese, so this may discourage you. But you'll be delighted if you ever get a chance to sample your very own.

Soured milk
Seasonings
Sweet cream

Take thick sour milk and simmer it slowly over a low heat until it thickens or coagulates into curd and the whey rises to the top. Strain through cheesecloth and let drip 6 hours before squeezing. Crumble to make a fine-grain cheese. Moisten with sweet cream and season to taste.

HEADCHEESE

Ingredients listed as needed.

I could start out by saying, "Take the head and feet of a pig," and you would close my book. Not many realize that headcheese is just about the nicest eating that a hog can offer you. Mother made it on the farm and, utilizing this part of the pig, nothing much was wasted, not even the tail. When making hot cakes she used it to grease the griddle. Why, Mother could never get along without this curly extremity. When the tail "ran short," Father knew it was butchering time again.

Mother always had someone clean the head, as the pig "didn't have a natural look, and this made me nervous," she ruefully said. But after the head was quartered, scrubbed, and cleaned and the ears chopped off, the feet were easy to do. She even polished the hooves—for sanitary reasons, so she said.

All day the meat was cooked in a big iron kettle with 1 cup of vinegar, 2 tablespoons of salt, and red pepper pods, adding more water if necessary. When the meat started to fall from the bones, Mom drained off the liquid and removed the skin, bones, and gristle. She then pulled the meat into small pieces until it was mushy, and seasoned it by adding 1 tablespoon of crushed mixed spices, ¼ teaspoon of red pepper, 2 tablespoons of black pepper, and 1 crushed bay leaf. If the flavor didn't come up to her expectations, she added this and that according to her taste. While the meat was still hot she pressed it firmly into bread pans, and she kept it chilled. If you don't think this is a real delicacy, ask your butcher the price per pound, for it takes a big head to make a little headcheese. To serve this, slice and garnish.

PICKLED NASTURTIUM SEEDS

A flower garden seasoning.

1 C. nasturtium seeds
White wine vinegar
2 tbsp. sugar
Pinch of cloves
¼ tsp. horseradish

Gather seeds when they are small and green. Let stand 3 days in salted water. Rinse in cold water and drain. Pack in ½-pint bottle. Add sugar, cloves, and horseradish. Pour in boiling vinegar. Cork at once. Use after 3 weeks.

SUGAR ROSE GARNISH

To decorate a sweetheart of a cake.

Egg white
Sweetheart rose
Granulated sugar

Beat egg white until frothy. Brush on rose with small artist's brush. Sprinkle with sugar. Allow to dry before placing on cake.

Salads

Mother wouldn't have known how to classify a gelatin square filled with canned fruit cocktail—not for her the nibble of lettuce! Her salads were beautiful and imaginative and planned to complement her main dish. A large clear glass bowl, her wedding gift from Cousin Annie, sat at Mother's right each dinner hour for as long as the farmhouse at Scio was home. From this crystal compote came the crisp greens, cucumbers, radishes, and onions blended with the Norton sweet-sour dressing. From this came the conglomerate of fruits, berries, and melons, chosen for color and ripeness. From this favorite bowl came dandelion greens with bacon and hard-boiled-egg slices or creamy cole slaw.

To Mama salads were not something you added to the menu because guests dropped in; they were an important part of our dinner. From July on, of course, the salad bowl was always augmented with a platter of solid red tomato slices.

A salad chef who had our farm products to choose from would have been in glory land. Leaf lettuce, vegetables, fruits from the orchard—all for the picking; nutmeats shelled and waiting in covered crocks; and in wintertime the canned treasures in the cellar!

BANANA SALAD

A filling salad when the entrée is light.

6 medium bananas
Mayonnaise
¾ C. finely chopped walnuts or peanuts
Lettuce leaves
Maraschino cherries

Peel bananas. Spread with mayonnaise. Roll in nuts. Place on lettuce leaves. Decorate with cherries. *Serves 6.*

CABBAGE, CARROT, AND RAISIN SALAD

Just to be different.

2 C. shredded cabbage
2 C. shredded carrots
1 C. raisins
1½ tsp. salt
⅔ C. mayonnaise
½ C. Old-Fashioned Boiled Dressing*

Mix salt, mayonnaise, and boiled dressing. Add to cabbage, carrots, and raisins. Toss until well mixed. *Serves 8 to 10.*

* See *Index.*

COOKED PRUNE SALAD

A diet delight.

  Prunes, cooked and pitted
  Cottage cheese
  Pineapple slices
  Lettuce
  Mayonnaise

Stuff prunes with cheese. Arrange with pineapple slices on lettuce leaves. Top with mayonnaise.

CRAB MEAT AND SHRIMP SALAD

Crisp texture for a summer day.

  1 medium green pepper, chopped
  1 medium onion, chopped
  1 C. chopped celery
  1 tsp. Worcestershire sauce
  ⅛ tsp. pepper
  1 can (6½ oz.) flaked crab meat
  1 can (6½ to 7 oz.) shrimp
  1 C. mayonnaise
  ½ tsp. salt

Blend all ingredients. Chill. Place in seashells. Sprinkle with paprika. *Serves 6 to 8.*

CRANBERRY SALAD

A tangy mold.

1 lb. fresh cranberries
1 whole orange cut into segments
2 packages strawberry gelatin
3 C. boiling water
- 1 C. diced celery
1 C. diced apples
½ C. chopped walnuts

Pour water over gelatin in a bowl, stirring until gelatin
is dissolved. Chill until slightly thickened. Put orange and
cranberries through food chopper. Add to gelatin mixture
along with celery, apples, and nuts. Put into desired mold.
Chill until firm. *Serves 8 to 10.*

CRANBERRY SAUCE SALAD

Bright and quick.

Jellied cranberry sauce, canned and chilled
Celery, chopped
Nuts, chopped
Mayonnaise

Slice cranberry sauce. Place on lettuce leaves. Top with
celery and nuts. Serve with mayonnaise.

CUCUMBER SALAD MOLD

Tingly cool green gelatin.

3 qt. boiling water
8 oz. lemon gelatin

2 tbsp. unflavored gelatin
1½ C. cold water
1 tbsp. salt
1 tsp. green food coloring
1 C. white vinegar
⅓ C. grated onion
2 tbsp. horseradish
3 cucumbers, grated with skins (medium blade)

Combine boiling water and lemon gelatin. Stir until dissolved. Combine unflavored gelatin with cold water and salt. Add to lemon gelatin mixture with food coloring and vinegar. Congeal over ice cubes until the consistency of unbeaten egg white. Fold in onion, horseradish, and cucumber. Pour into greased molds. Refrigerate until set.

GERMAN COLE SLAW

I am indebted to Frieda for this.

1½ tsp. salt
¼ tsp. pepper
¾ C. sugar
¼ C. white vinegar
4 C. medium ground cabbage
4 slices crisp bacon, chopped
3 tbsp. hot bacon grease

Mix salt, pepper, sugar, and vinegar. Fold in cabbage. Chill for 3 hours. Drain. Put in serving dish. Top with bacon. Pour hot bacon grease on top. Serve immediately. *Serves 6.*

GREEN BEAN SALAD

All cool green with a speck of color.

2 C. cooked green beans, drained
¼ C. diced celery
¼ C. slivered green pepper
¼ C. chopped green garden onions
2 tbsp. chopped pimento
¼ tsp. salt
⅓ C. French dressing

Mix all ingredients lightly. *Serves 6.*

GREEN MOUNTAIN SALAD MOLD

A company favorite.

2 packages lime gelatin
1½ C. boiling water
2 C. pineapple juice
2 C. heavy cream, whipped
2 C. crushed pineapple, drained
2 packages cream cheese (3 oz. each)

Add boiling water to gelatin. Stir until dissolved. Add pineapple juice. Put in refrigerator until the consistency of egg white. Whip cream cheese and gelatin. Fold in pineapple and cream. Mold. Chill. *Serves 10 to 12.*

HOLIDAY CRANBERRY SALAD

For the festive mood.

1 lb. cranberries
1 qt. water
¼ tsp. salt
¼ tsp. baking soda
2 C. sugar
2 small packages strawberry gelatin
2 C. miniature marshmallows
1 C. chopped celery
2 C. chopped apples
1 C. walnuts

Bring cranberries, water, and salt to a boil. Add soda and cook 10 minutes. Add sugar, gelatin, and marshmallows while still hot. Let cool. Add celery, apples, and walnuts. Pour into desired mold. *Chill 4 hours.*

KANDY'S SALAD MEDLEY

The appeal of this salad is the perfect marriage of unusual ingredients. However, any 12 or more items will produce a delicious blend.

Avocado	Tomato	Celery
Artichoke	Fresh mushrooms	Peach
Grapes	Apple	Green pepper
Cauliflowerets	Green beans	Mangoes
Croutons	Asparagus	Black olives
Carrots	Cucumber	Hard-cooked egg
Peeled citrus fruit	Onion	Watercress
Spinach	Salted nuts	Crisp, chopped bacon

Choose 12 or more varieties. Cut in medium pieces to
make 10 cups all together. Toss with Dietrich's Salad
Dressing.* Serve in large Burgundy wine glasses. *Serves
8 to 10.*

MACARONI, TUNA, AND PEA SALAD

For that hot summer day.

  1 package (7 oz.) shell macaroni
  1 can (7 oz.) tuna, drained
  1 can sweet peas, drained
  1 tbsp. celery seed
  2 tbsp. choppel stuffed olives
  2 tbsp. diced sweet pickles

DRESSING:
  1 C. mayonnaise
  ½ tsp. salt
  ¼ tsp. pepper
  ¼ tsp. garlic powder

Cook macaroni as directed on package. Drain and rinse
with cold water. Add remaining ingredients. Mix dressing
and stir into macaroni mixture. Chill. *Serves 6 to 8.*

MARINATED BEAN SALAD

For your next picnic.

  1½ C. green beans
  1½ C. yellow beans
  1½ C. kidney beans
  1½ C. garbanzo beans
  1 green pepper, cut up
  1 large sweet onion, sliced

* See *Index.*

DRESSING:

½ C. sugar
½ C. salad oil
½ C. wine vinegar
½ tsp. salt

Drain beans. Combine dressing ingredients. Pour over beans, pepper, and onion. Marinate overnight, in refrigerator. *Serves 12.*

MIXED BEAN SALAD

Use it on your next Saturday night buffet.

1½ C. kidney beans, drained
1 C. chopped celery
½ C. chopped sweet pickles
¼ C. chopped sweet onion
¼ C. yellow cooked string beans, cut in 1-inch pieces
2 tbsp. chopped pimento
¼ C. sweet pickle juice

Combine all together and marinate 1 hour before serving. Toss lightly in French dressing. Serve in bowl lined with cabbage or lettuce leaves. Garnish with hard-cooked-egg slices. *Serves 6.*

OLD-FASHIONED CABBAGE SALAD

From Grandma's days.

  1 qt. medium chopped cabbage
  ¼ C. chopped green pepper
  ¼ C. chopped pimento
  ¼ C. chopped onion
  1½ recipes of Cabbage Dressing*

Toss all ingredients into cabbage dressing. Serve on lettuce cups. *Serves 6 to 8.*

OLD-TIME KIDNEY BEAN SALAD

Another variation.

  2½ C. kidney beans, drained
  1½ C. chopped celery
  ½ C. chopped sweet pickle
  ¼ C. chopped onion
  ⅓ C. French dressing

Combine ingredients and toss lightly with dressing. Chill. *Serves 6 to 8.*

SEASHORE SALAD

Take it on your next beach picnic.

SALAD
  3 qt. boiling water
  1 tbsp. salt
  4 oz. shell macaroni
  ¾ C. flaked salmon

* See *Index.*

½ C. diced celery
½ C. diced sweet pickles

DRESSING:
½ C. salad dressing
½ C. mayonnaise
¼ tsp. salt
1 tsp. sugar
1 tsp. celery salt
¼ C. evaporated milk

Add salt to boiling water. Gradually add shell macaroni.
Cook until tender, approximately 10 minutes. Drain.
Rinse in cold water. Prepare dressing by blending ingredients. Arrange alternating bands of macaroni and salmon
mixture on platter with lettuce or other crisp greens. Pour
dressing over macaroni. Sprinkle with paprika. Chill.
Serves 4 to 6.

SOUR CREAM COLE SLAW

Refreshing for days of soaring temperatures.

½ medium head of cabbage
½ C. sour cream
2 tbsp. vinegar
½ tsp. salt
⅛ tsp. pepper
2 tbsp. sugar

Chill cabbage thoroughly. Shred fine. Measure out about
4 cups. Combine remaining ingredients and pour over
cabbage. Mix lightly. Sprinkle with paprika. Variation:
For extra flavor, 1½ teaspoons whole celery seed, ¼ cup
shredded green peppers, or ⅓ cup crushed, drained pineapple may be added. *Serves 6 to 8.*

TURKEY AND PINEAPPLE SALAD

For the first Sunday supper after Christmas.

2 C. diced turkey
½ C. diced celery
½ C. pineapple tidbits, well drained
¼ C. sliced toasted almonds
¼ C. mayonnaise
¼ C. Old-Fashioned Boiled Dressing*
½ tsp. salt
¼ tsp. pepper

Combine turkey, celery, pineapple, and almonds in a bowl. Mix boiled dressing, mayonnaise, salt, and pepper. Toss with all ingredients, until coated. Chill. *Serves 6 to 8.*

VEGETABLE SALAD

Colorful, tart, and trim.

Fresh spinach
Beets
Green beans
French dressing

Mix vegetables and toss with French dressing.

* See *Index*

WALDORF SALAD

Variations below.

3 C. diced apples
1 C. diced celery
½ tsp. sugar
⅓ C. Old-Fashioned Boiled Dressing*
¾ C. heavy cream, whipped

Mix sugar, cream, and boiled dressing. Pour over apples
and celery, and toss. Chill. *Serves 6 to 8.* Variations:
Substitute grapefruit or orange segments, pineapple
chunks, or grapes for apples.

WATERMELON BOWL

A festival of fruits.

Cut watermelon lengthwise in a ⅓ to ⅔ proportion.
Remove top ⅓. Cut out melon balls with a French vegetable cutter. Chill. Mark off 2-inch spaces on cut edge of
melon and cut out triangular sections between each
marker, making a notched edge. Fill bowl with chilled
watermelon, cantaloupe balls, and other fresh fruits.

* See *Index*.

Salad Dressings

CABBAGE DRESSING

Delightfully different flavor.

    1 tbsp. cider vinegar
    ½ C. Old-Fashioned Boiled Dressing*
    ½ C. mayonnaise
    ¼ tsp. pepper
    1 tbsp. sugar
    1 tsp. salt

Mix all ingredients. Cover. Refrigerate. *Makes 1 cup.*

CREAMY FRENCH DRESSING

A universal favorite.

    2 eggs
    ¼ tsp. garlic powder
    2 tbsp. sugar

* See *Index.*

1 tbsp. salt
1 tsp. paprika
½ tsp. dry mustard
2 tsp. Worcestershire sauce
1½ C. catsup
¼ C. mayonnaise
2 C. salad oil
½ C. vinegar
½ C. warm water

Beat eggs until fluffy, about 4 minutes. Add garlic powder, sugar, salt, paprika, mustard, Worcestershire sauce, catsup, and mayonnaise. Beat until creamy. Add oil slowly while mixing. Continue with vinegar and water. Beat for 5 minutes. *Makes 5 cups.*

CURRY DRESSING

For fresh greens.

1 C. tarragon vinegar
1 C. olive oil
2 C. corn oil
1 tbsp. dry mustard
1 tbsp. curry powder
3 tbsp. MSG
2 eggs
1 tbsp. salt

Beat in mixer 5 minutes at high speed. *Makes 4½ cups.*

DIETRICH'S SALAD DRESSING

Keep on hand in refrigerator.

2 tbsp. lemon juice
2 tbsp. wine vinegar
½ tsp. dry mustard
1 C. olive oil
1 tbsp. MSG
1 tsp. salt
½ tsp. freshly ground black pepper

Mix all together in pint jar. Shake 1 minute. Store in refrigerator.

FARMER'S DAUGHTER DRESSING

A success in Orland Park as well as in Scio County.

½ C. finely chopped garlic cloves
½ C. finely chopped onion
2 tbsp. salt
⅓ C. sugar
1 tsp. prepared mustard
1 tsp. white pepper
1 qt. salad oil
3 C. white vinegar

Beat ingredients except oil and vinegar to a thick paste, approximately 10 minutes. Add 1 cup oil until mixture emulsifies. Add oil and vinegar alternately, beating vigorously. *Makes 2 quarts.*

FARMER'S DAUGHTER
THOUSAND ISLAND DRESSING

Our famous recipe.

½ C. mayonnaise
½ C. boiled dressing
1½ C. chili sauce
¼ tsp. salt
1½ tbsp. sugar

Mix all together. *Makes 2½ cups.*

FLUFFY PINK DRESSING

A topper for your fruit salad platter.

1 C. mayonnaise
1 C. jellied cranberry sauce
¼ tsp. salt
½ C. heavy cream, whipped

Blend mayonnaise, cranberry sauce, and salt. Fold in whipped cream. Spoon over fruit. *Makes 2½ to 3 cups.*

GARLIC DRESSING NUMBER ONE

Worth all the ingredients.

¾ C. salad oil
¼ C. hot water
2 tbsp. wine vinegar
¼ C. sweet pickle juice
½ tsp. dry mustard
½ tsp. salt
¼ tsp. pepper

¼ tsp. celery salt
1 clove garlic, minced
1 tbsp. sugar
⅛ tsp. paprika
2 tbsp. lemon juice
2 tbsp. Worcestershire sauce
1 tsp. oregano

Blend all ingredients in blender. Store in jar. Refrigerate. *Makes 1¾ cups.*

GARLIC DRESSING NUMBER TWO

A mellower touch.

1 C. oil
½ C. wine vinegar
1 tsp. thyme
1 tsp. oregano
1 tsp. garlic juice
¼ C. sweet pickle juice
¼ C. sweet fruit juice
½ tsp. salt
¼ tsp. pepper
1 tbsp. honey

Mix all together and shake vigorously. *Makes 2 cups.*

HOMEMADE MAYONNAISE

Aunt Leah's.

1 tsp. prepared mustard
1 tsp. dry mustard
1 tsp. salt
1 tsp. sugar

⅔ C. egg yolks
3 tbsp. lemon juice
3 tbsp. vinegar
1½ qt. cold salad oil

Combine mustards, salt, sugar, and egg yolks. Beat at high speed until light and fluffy. Add lemon juice and vinegar. Dribble in oil slowly while still mixing. When smooth, pour into jar. Refrigerate. *Makes 1¾ quarts.*

OLD-FASHIONED BOILED SALAD DRESSING

Excellent to use in Thousand Island Dressing.

⅔ C. margarine
2 C. sifted all-purpose flour
⅔ C. sugar
2 tbsp. dry mustard
1½ C. vinegar
3 C. water
1½ C. egg yolk
2 tbsp. salt

Melt margarine. Add flour, and cook thoroughly. Combine sugar and mustard with 1 cup water and ½ cup vinegar. Add slowly to hot mixture and stir. Add rest of vinegar and water. Cook 5 minutes. Beat egg yolk and salt slightly. Stir into mixture. Bring to a boil, stirring constantly until thick. If lumpy, beat with mixer until smooth. Cool. Put into jar. Refrigerate. *Makes approximately 1¾ quarts.*

PINEAPPLE CREAM DRESSING

To accent a fruit plate.

3 egg yolks
½ C. sugar
¼ C. lemon juice
½ C. pineapple juice
¼ tsp. salt
1 C. heavy cream, chilled and whipped

Put egg yolks, sugar, lemon, pineapple juices, and salt in double boiler. Cook until mixture thickens. Cool. Fold in whipped cream and beat lightly until smooth. *Makes 2 cups.* Variation: Substitute orange for pineapple juice.

RUSSIAN DRESSING

A heady flavor for tossed greens.

1 C. mayonnaise
⅓ C. catsup
⅓ C. chili sauce
2 tbsp. prepared mustard
1 tsp. sugar
½ tsp. salt

Blend all ingredients. *Makes 1¾ cups.*

TARRAGON DRESSING

Slightly piquant.

1 C. tomato sauce
½ C. tarragon vinegar
2 tsp. salt
½ tsp. paprika
1 tbsp. Worcestershire sauce
1 C. salad oil
¼ C. sugar
½ tsp. pepper
½ tsp. prepared mustard
Small clove garlic, cut up
Small onion, quartered
3 tbsp. horseradish

Blend all together in blender. Keep in covered jar in refrigerator. *Makes 2½ cups.*

Breads and Rolls

Every Friday morning Mother took an accountable pride in "getting up with the chickens" to be at her queenly task of bread making. There were never less than eight loaves, and this was a ritual that was repeated during the week if she ran short. She often did, for our farmhouse was a hub for community gatherings and drop-by guests.

When the loaves first came from the oven, we were always tantalized into cutting thick slices that disappeared under the weight of jam and freshly churned butter. Mother never scolded, and she often joined us with a pot of hot cocoa or cinnamon tea.

Pictures fill my head of long pantry shelves lined with daisy oilcloth and eight loaves of bread laid on their sides to cool. Suddenly there are seven. Mother's only comment: "You children will spoil your supper." Then she would turn smilingly aside, knowing that number seven was about to fall to the assault of her greedy youngsters.

Quick Breads

AUNT DILLY'S DATE AND NUT BREAD

Her claim to a deserved fame.

¾ C. chopped pecans
1 C. chopped dates
1½ tsp. baking soda
¼ C. soft butter
½ tsp. salt
¾ C. boiling water
2 eggs, beaten slightly
1 tsp. vanilla
1 C. sugar
1½ C. sifted all-purpose flour

Combine pecans, dates, soda, butter, salt, and boiling water. Allow this mixture to stand for 15 minutes. Beat in eggs, vanilla, sugar, and flour. Don't overmix. Put batter into greased and floured loaf pan (9 x 5 x 3 inches). Bake in preheated oven (350°F.) approximately 70 to 80 minutes. Cool 10 minutes. Loosen sides with spatula. Place loaf on cake rack to cool for 2 hours.

BAKING SODA BREAD

A bit of Irish.

2 eggs
¼ C. butter, melted
1 C. buttermilk
2 C. sifted cake flour
2 tsp. baking powder
½ C. sugar
1 tsp. salt

¼ tsp. baking soda
1 C. chopped nuts

Blend eggs, butter, and buttermilk. Combine dry ingredients. Mix in with egg mixture until smooth. Stir in nuts. Pour batter into greased and floured loaf pan (9 x 5 x 3 inches). Let rest 20 minutes. Bake in preheated oven (350°F.) for 60 to 75 minutes. *Makes 1 loaf.*

BANANA NUT BREAD

Breakfast-brunch distinction.

¼ C. margarine
¾ C. sugar
1 egg
⅔ C. mashed bananas
1¾ C. all-purpose flour
½ tsp. baking powder
¼ tsp. salt
½ tsp. soda
3 tbsp. sour milk or buttermilk
½ C. chopped nuts

Cream margarine, sugar, and egg. Stir in mashed bananas. Combine dry ingredients. Add to creamed mixture alternately with milk. Stir in nuts. Pour into greased loaf pan (9 x 5 x 3 inches). Bake in preheated oven (350°F.) for 75 to 90 minutes.

BLUEBERRY HILL MUFFINS

A patch of blueberries sweet and mild,
My favorite spot when I was a child.

   ½ C. margarine
   1¼ C. sugar
   2 eggs
   1 C. commercial sour cream
   1 tsp. vanilla
   2 C. sifted all-purpose flour
   1 tsp. baking powder
   ½ tsp. soda
   ¼ tsp. salt
   ½ C. blueberries

Cream margarine and sugar. Add eggs and beat until smooth. Mix in sour cream and vanilla. Combine dry ingredients. Stir into creamed mixture. Fold in blueberries. Spoon into muffin tins that have been lined with crinkle cups or greased and floured, filling ½ full. Bake in preheated oven (400°F.) for approximately 25 to 30 minutes. *Makes 2 dozen*. Dust muffins with confectioners' sugar when they are cooled, or just before serving if they are to be served warm.

BUTTERMILK GRIDDLE CAKES

Make them on an iron spider.

   1 C. buttermilk
   ½ C. heavy cream
   2 eggs
   1½ C. sifted all-purpose flour
   1 tsp. baking powder
   ½ tsp. soda

½ tsp. salt
¼ tsp. sugar
¼ C. butter, melted

Beat eggs. Add buttermilk and cream. Sift dry ingredients. Combine with egg mixture. Beat until smooth. Stir in butter. *Makes 6 to 8.*

CANDIED FRUIT BREAD

Christmas holiday delight.

4 C. sifted all-purpose flour
2 tbsp. baking powder
½ tsp. salt
1½ C. sugar
½ C. chopped candied citron
½ C. currants
½ C. chopped candied red cherries
½ C. chopped candied green cherries
1 C. chopped nuts
4 eggs, beaten
2 C. milk
⅓ C. butter, melted

Sift dry ingredients. Add fruit and nuts. Combine eggs, milk, and butter. Add to flour mixture. Stir until blended. Push batter into 2 greased loaf pans (9 x 5 x 3 inches). Bake in preheated oven (375°F.) for 1 hour.

CINNAMONY RAISIN TOAST

A morning treat for a sweet tooth.

Toast one side of raisin cinnamon bread. Generously butter side not toasted. Sprinkle with 2 tablespoons cinnamon-and-sugar mixture. Slide under broiler until bubbly. Serve immediately. Allow 1 to 2 slices per person.

COFFEE CAKE MUFFINS

Perfect for a neighborly coffee break.

½ C. brown sugar, packed
½ C. chopped walnuts
2 tbsp. flour
2 tsp. cinnamon
2 tbsp. butter, melted
1½ C. sifted all-purpose flour
½ C. sugar
2 tsp. baking powder
1 tsp. salt
¼ C. margarine
1 egg, beaten
½ C. milk

Combine brown sugar, walnuts, 2 tablespoons flour, cinnamon, and butter. Set mixture aside. Cut margarine into 1½ cup flour, sugar, baking powder, and salt until mixture resembles coarse crumbs. Add egg and milk to mixture. Stir until flour is moist. Spoon batter into greased muffin tins alternately with the nut mixture, filling pans ⅔ full. Bake in preheated oven (400°F) for approximately 25 to 30 minutes. *Makes 1 dozen.*

COUNTRY FRIED MUSH

A winter breakfast down on the farm.

1 C. yellow cornmeal
1 tsp. salt
1 C. cold water
3 C. boiling water

Combine cornmeal, salt, and cold water. Stir mixture into boiling water. Cook 10 minutes, covered. Rinse 2-pound loaf pan with water. Pour batter into pan. Cool 1 hour and refrigerate overnight. Turn out and cut into ½-inch slices. Dip in flour. Fry on hot, greased griddle until brown on both sides. Pass the syrup. *Serves 4 hungry farmhands.*

CREAM OF TARTAR BISCUITS

Gran scorned baking powder.

¼ C. shortening
3 C. sifted cake flour
½ tsp. salt
1½ tsp. cream of tartar
¾ tsp. soda
1 C. milk

Cut shortening into flour, salt, and cream of tartar. Dissolve soda in milk. Mix with dry ingredients. Roll out on floured board and handle lightly. Cut with biscuit cutter. Don't always cut your biscuits the usual way, but take a knife and cut in different shapes and sizes to suit your mood and needs. Try a square, or something else. For crusty biscuits space them so sides do not touch on the baking sheet; for soft sides, have biscuits touching. A very hot oven to start with will make your biscuits puff high. Bake in preheated oven (450°F.) for 12 to 15 minutes. *Makes about 1 dozen.*

CRÊPES FOR SOUP

To sophisticate a broth.

    1 egg
    ½ C. sifted all-purpose flour
    Dash of salt
    ¼ C. milk
    ¼ C. cooled chicken broth
    1 tbsp. butter, melted

Beat egg. Add rest of ingredients. Mix well. Drop by spoonfuls onto hot griddle. Cool and cut into thin strips. *Makes approximately 1½ cups.* Refrigerate until ready to use. Good in bouillon or thin types of soups.

CRÊPES, WAFFLES, OR PANCAKES

Versatile batter.

    1 C. sour cream
    1 C. coffee cream
    8 egg yolks
    ½ C. butter, melted and cooked to a light golden color
    2 C. sifted cake flour
    ¼ tsp. salt
    ½ tsp. baking powder
    8 egg whites
    3 tbsp. sugar

Mix sour cream, coffee cream, yolks, and butter. Sift dry ingredients and add to cream mixture. Beat egg whites and sugar until stiff but not dry. Fold egg whites into batter until well blended. Make crêpes in 6- to 8-inch skillet, lightly greasing pan after each use. *Makes 30 6-inch crêpes.* Variation: For pancakes or waffles, increase flour by ½ cup. Pancakes or waffles may be sprinkled with blueberries or sliced strawberries before being turned on griddle.

DROP DUMPLINGS

Serve with stews.

2 C. sifted cake flour
3 tbsp. baking powder
1 tsp. salt
¼ C. lard
1 tbsp. dried parsley
1 tbsp. grated onion
1 scant C. milk

Sift dry ingredients. Cut in lard until it looks like coarse meal. Stir in parsley, onions, and milk. Mix well. Drop by tablespoonfuls on a flat perforated steamer that has water boiling in it. (I made one by punching holes an inch apart in an 8-inch round cake tin and placing it over a pot filled with 2 inches of water.) Cover with lid; don't peek for 15 minutes. *Makes 10 medium-sized dumplings.* Hint: When made this way, they will not have a tendency to be soggy.

FLAT BREAD

To serve with your favorite soup.

4½ C. sifted all-purpose flour
⅓ C. sugar
4 tsp. baking powder
1 tsp. salt
½ C. wheat germ
1 C. whole wheat flour
¼ C. margarine
1½ C. milk
½ C. molasses
¼ C. poppy or sesame seeds

Set aside ½ cup flour. Combine dry ingredients except
seeds. Cut in margarine until mixture is mealy. Mix milk
and molasses. Add to flour mixture and beat until blended.
Put ½ cup flour on board, and knead dough until flour is
absorbed. Pinch off approximately 20 snippets of dough
(¾-inch balls). Sprinkle board with seeds and place balls
on top. Roll dough as thin and as round as possible. Place
bread on greased and floured baking sheet 1 inch apart.
Bake in preheated oven (350°F.) for 10 to 15 minutes.
Let cool and stack. *Makes approximately 20.*

FRENCH FRIED TOAST

Crunchy and golden breakfast slices.

½ C. egg yolks
½ C. coffee cream
½ tsp. salt
2-day-old bread slices, cut in half
Finely crushed cornflakes
Confectioners' sugar

Beat egg yolks, coffee cream, and salt. Dip bread in mixture and then in cornflakes. Deep fry (375°F.) until golden. Sprinkle with confectioners' sugar.

GOLD TOAST

A regal breakfast.

    ½ C. evaporated milk
    ¼ tsp. salt
    1 egg
    ½ tsp. vanilla
    2-day-old bread slices
    Confectioners' sugar

Mix milk, salt, egg, and vanilla. Beat 1 minute. Dip bread slices in mixture. Deep fry (375°F.) until golden. Sprinkle with confectioners' sugar.

JOHNNY CAKE

An everyday quick bread for the kids.

    ½ C. margarine
    ⅓ C. sugar
    2 eggs
    1¾ C. buttermilk
    1 C. yellow cornmeal
    1 C. sifted all-purpose flour
    2 tsp. baking powder
    ¾ tsp. salt
    ¾ tsp. baking soda

Cream margarine and sugar. Beat in eggs. Add buttermilk. Mix all dry ingredients. Add to creamed mixture.

Pour batter into greased and floured pan (8 x 8 x 2 inches). Bake in preheated oven (375°F.) for 30 to 40 minutes. Serve warm with plenty of butter. *Serves 8 to 10.*

LEMON BREAD

For that afternoon tea.

1 C. sugar
6 tbsp. butter
1 tsp. baking powder
Rind of 1 lemon, grated
1½ C. sifted all-purpose flour
½ C. milk
2 eggs, separated
¼ tsp. salt
½ C. chopped walnuts
½ C. chopped candied red cherries
Juice of 1 lemon
¼ tsp. lemon extract
⅓ C. sugar

Cream 1 cup sugar and butter. Combine baking powder, lemon rind, and flour. Add to creamed mixture alternately with milk. Beat in egg yolks until smooth. Fold in beaten egg whites that have been whipped with salt. Fold in nuts and cherries. Pour batter into greased and floured loaf pan (10 x 5 x 3 inches). Bake in preheated oven (375°F.) for approximately 1 hour. Combine lemon juice, extract, and ⅓ cup sugar in saucepan. Simmer 1 minute and cool slightly. Pour over hot bread. Let cool and cut as desired.

OLD-FASHIONED BAKING POWDER BISCUITS

Fond memories of when Mom served them topped with wild strawberries.

⅓ C. lard
2 C. sifted cake flour
¾ tsp. salt
4 tsp. baking powder
1 tbsp. sugar
½ C. cool milk
½ tbsp. bacon drippings

Blend lard into dry ingredients until the size of a pea. Add milk and drippings. Stir vigorously for 1 minute. Turn out on floured board and knead slightly. Roll to ¾-inch thickness. Cut with 2-inch cutter. Place on ungreased baking sheet ⅛ inch apart. Brush with butter. Let rest 15 minutes. Bake in preheated oven (425°F.) for 20 minutes. *Makes 8 biscuits.*

OLD-FASHIONED BROWN BREAD

Mom's favorite.

1 tbsp. butter
½ C. sugar
½ C. molasses
1 C. sifted all-purpose flour
1 C. graham or wheat flour
1 tsp. soda
1 tsp. salt
1 C. buttermilk
½ C. raisins*

Cream butter and sugar. Stir in molasses. Combine dry ingredients. Add to creamed mixture alternately with buttermilk. Beat just until smooth. Add raisins, if desired. Pour into greased loaf pan (9 x 5 x 3 inches). Bake in preheated oven (375°F.) for 45 to 50 minutes, or until done. Cool 10 minutes. Take out of pan and set bread on its side on rack to finish cooling. Don't forget the baked beans.

OLD-TIME WAFFLE BATTER

And variations.

    ½ C. egg yolks, beaten
    2½ C. coffee cream
    2¼ C. sifted cake flour
    2½ tbsp. baking powder
    ¼ tsp. salt
    ½ C. sugar
    ¾ C. egg whites, beaten

Combine egg yolk and cream. Sift dry ingredients. Add to yolk mixture. Fold in egg white. Pour into hot waffle iron. Bake 4 to 5 minutes. Variations: (1) For Black Walnut Waffles, add ¾ cup black walnuts to batter and stir. (2) For Apple Waffles, fold in 1 cup peeled and diced apples. (3) For Cheese Waffles, fold in ¾ cup grated cheese. (4) For Blueberry or Sliced Strawberry Waffles, sprinkle 1 heaping tablespoon of berries on top of waffles before closing lid. *Makes 6 to 8 waffles.*

* Optional.

PLAIN POPOVERS

Delicious with butter or jelly.

6 eggs, slightly beaten
2 C. warm milk
⅓ C. butter, melted
2 C. sifted all-purpose flour
1 tsp. salt

Mix all ingredients until blended. Pour into 12 greased custard cups (6 ounces). Place cups on a pan for easier handling. Bake in preheated oven (450°F.) for 30 minutes. Cut slit in side of each. Lower oven temperature to 350°F. and bake 15 to 20 minutes longer. Serve hot.

POPOVERS

Foolproof, like an English nanny.

½ C. eggs
1 C. sifted all-purpose flour
1 tsp. salt
1 C. milk

Beat eggs 1 minute. Add remaining ingredients. Mix until smooth. Pour into heavily greased popover pan, filling ½ full. Bake in preheated oven (425°F.) for 30 minutes. Reduce heat to 250°F. and continue baking for about 20 minutes. Cut slit in side to let out steam. Turn oven off and leave door open until you are ready to use popovers. *Makes 10 to 12.*

POTATO BISCUITS

Use up your yesterday's mashed potatoes.

1¼ C. sifted all-purpose flour
½ tsp. salt
4 tsp. baking powder
2 tbsp. lard
½ C. cold mashed potatoes
½ C. milk
Soft butter

Mix dry ingredients. Cut in lard and mashed potatoes until mixture looks like meal. (Use fingertips or pastry blender.) Stir in enough milk to make a soft dough. On a floured board knead dough gently for 1 minute. Roll to ½-inch thick and cut with 1½- or 2-inch biscuit cutter. Place on ungreased baking sheet. Brush with soft butter. Bake in preheated oven (450°F.) for 10 to 12 minutes. *Makes 1 dozen.*

SOUR CREAM COFFEE CAKE

Sugar 'n' spice and ever'thing.

BATTER
½ C. margarine
1¼ C. sugar
2 eggs
1 C. commercial sour cream
1 tsp. vanilla
2 C. sifted cake flour
½ tsp. soda
¼ tsp. salt

FILLING AND TOPPING

⅓ C. sugar
1 tbsp. cinnamon
¾ tsp. mace
3 tbsp. butter, melted
1¼ C. chopped walnuts

Cream margarine and sugar until light and fluffy. Add eggs and beat well. Mix in sour cream and vanilla. Sift dry ingredients and stir into batter until smooth. Pour ½ of the batter into a greased and floured square (9 inch) pan. Mix all ingredients of the filling and topping together. Spread ½ of mixture on the batter. Pour remaining batter over topping mixture. Spread remaining topping mixture on top of batter. Bake in preheated oven (350°F.) for 45 minutes. *Makes 10 to 12 servings.*

SOUR DOUGH PANCAKES

As only Kirby can make them.

2 C. Sour Dough Starter*
1 tbsp. butter, melted
⅓ C. sifted all-purpose flour
2 tbsp. sugar
2 eggs, beaten
½ tsp. salt
1 tsp. baking soda
1 drop yellow food coloring

Combine all ingredients in mixer and beat 1 minute, or until smooth. Store batter overnight in refrigerator. Let batter stand at room temperature 15 minutes before making up. Stir. Use ¼-cup measuring cup to pour batter on lightly greased hot griddle. Brown, turning once. *Makes 8 to 10 5-inch pancakes.*

* See *Index.*

SOUTHERN HUSH PUPPIES

It all started when a cook threw out cornmeal balls fried in fish oil to the yelping dogs, saying, "Hush, puppy."

1 C. yellow cornmeal
2 tsp. baking powder
½ tsp. salt
¼ tsp. white pepper
2 eggs, beaten
¼ C. milk
¼ C. minced onion

Combine all ingredients and beat until well mixed. Flour hands and make 1-inch balls. Fry in deep fat (350°F.) for about 3 to 5 minutes. *Makes 10 balls.* Serve with butter. Good with river catfish (fresh or frozen).

TEN O'CLOCK PANCAKES

For that lazy, late Sunday morning.

4 eggs, separated
1 tsp. salt
1⅔ C. milk
1½ C. sifted all-purpose flour
2 tbsp. sugar
⅔ C. butter, melted

Beat egg whites and salt until stiff. Mix egg yolks and milk. Add to flour and sugar. Stir in butter. Fold in egg whites. Bake on lightly greased griddle until golden, turning once. *Makes enough for a hungry 6.*

WHEAT GEMS

Early breakfast favorite.

  1 C. sifted all-purpose flour
  1 C. wheat flour
  ½ C. sugar
  2 tsp. baking powder
  ½ tsp. salt
  1 tsp. baking soda
  ½ C. buttermilk
  ½ C. sweet milk
  1 egg, beaten
  ⅓ C. butter, melted

Combine dry ingredients. Mix in buttermilk, sweet milk, egg, and butter. Fill greased muffin cups ⅔ full. Bake in preheated oven (400°F.) for 20 to 25 minutes. *Makes 16 muffins.*

SPAETZELS

Like noodles, serve them in chicken soup or fry them in butter and use as a meat accompaniment.

  1 C. boiling water
  ½ C. butter
  2½ C. flour
  4 eggs
  ½ tsp. salt
  2 qt. chicken stock

Pour boiling water into mixer bowl. Add butter. When melted, beat in flour and salt. Add eggs, one at a time. Beat well after each addition. Bring stock to boil. Put dumpling batter into spaetzel maker. Hold over stock and let batter drip through. Boil 3 minutes. Remove dumplings with a slotted spoon and place them in a large pot of ice water. Cool 10 minutes. Drain and place on towels. *Makes approximately 4 cups.*

Yeast Breads
BACKYARD CLOTHSPIN ROLLS

Country bumpkin goodness.

Use basic Sweet Dough recipe.* Roll dough to ¼ inch thick, in rectangular shape. Brush with butter. Fold over once. Cut into strips ½ inch wide and 8 inches long. Grease wooden clothespins. Wrap strip around each. Put on greased cookie sheets. Bake in preheated oven (375°F.) for 15 to 20 minutes. Rolls should be light, golden color. *Makes 40 rolls.* Serve on clothespins in bun basket lined with red and white checked napkin.

BASIC SWEET DOUGH

One dough for a dozen variations.

2 tbsp. dry yeast
¼ C. warm water

* See *Index*.

1 C. hot milk
2 tbsp. sugar
2 tsp. salt
½ C. butter
5 C. sifted all-purpose flour
2 eggs
Salad oil

Dissolve yeast in warm water and set aside. Add sugar, salt, and butter to the hot milk. Cool to lukewarm. Beat in 3 cups flour. Add yeast and eggs, and continue to beat for 3 minutes. Beat in with a wooden spoon enough additional flour to make a dough that is not sticky. Turn out on floured board and knead until satiny. Place in greased bowl and brush top with salad oil. Let rise until double. Punch down and repeat rising. Turn out and let rest 10 minutes. Shape as desired. Variations: (1) For Cloverleafs, make up dough in 1-inch balls, and place 3 balls in each greased muffin tin; brush with butter; let rise until double; bake in preheated oven (375°F.) for 25 to 30 minutes. *Makes 2 dozen.* (2) For Fan Tans, roll dough into rectangle ⅓ inch thick; spread with soft butter; cut crosswise into 6 strips, about 1½ inches in width; stack evenly and cut into 20 to 24 pieces about 1 inch wide; place cut side down in greased muffin tins; bake in preheated oven (375°F.) for 25 to 30 minutes.

BLACK BREAD

So big a loaf you have never seen.

2 tbsp. dry yeast
2⅔ C. warm water
2 tbsp. salt
¼ C. soft shortening
¾ C. caramel coloring (buy it at the bakery)
2 tbsp. anise seed
2 tbsp. caraway seed
2⅔ C. medium rye flour
6 C. sifted all-purpose flour
Cornmeal
1 tbsp. caraway seed*

Dissolve yeast in ⅓ cup warm water. Add the rest of the water, salt, soft shortening, coloring and anise and caraway seeds. Beat in rye and all-purpose flours. Knead until smooth and elastic. Put into lightly greased bowl. Cover with clean cloth. Set in warm place to rise until doubled in bulk. Punch down. Let rise 45 minutes. Turn out onto lightly floured surface. Shape into large ball. Place on baking sheet which has been sprinkled with cornmeal. Let rise one-half as much. Sprinkle with additional caraway seed, if desired. Bake in preheated oven (375°F.) for 45 to 50 minutes. Brush with Starch Glaze† while hot.

* Optional.
† See Index.

BLACK-EYED SUSAN BREAD

As welcome as the first wild blooms of May.

½ C. margarine, melted
½ C. sugar
2 tsp. salt
2 eggs, beaten
1 tbsp. dry yeast
½ C. warm water
2 C. milk, scalded
6½ to 7 C. sifted all-purpose flour
1 C. dark seedless raisins
1 tsp. cinnamon

Dissolve sugar and salt in margarine. Stir in eggs. Soften yeast in warm water. Add to egg mixture. Cool milk to lukewarm. Add to mixture. Beat in 5 cups flour for 4 minutes. With a wooden spoon, beat in 1 cup flour, raisins, and cinnamon. Add enough additional flour to make it easy to handle, and knead for 3 minutes. Place dough into greased bowl and cover. Let rise in warm place until doubled. Punch down and let rest 10 minutes. Divide dough into 3 parts. Grease 2 loaf pans (9 x 5 x 3 inches), and shape dough into each. Grease 1 square pan 8 x 8 x 2 inches), and make up third part of the dough into rolls. Cover and let rise until dough is to the rim. Bake in preheated oven (375°F.) for approximately 50 minutes for bread, and 40 minutes for rolls. Remove bread and let rest on its side on rack until cool. Ice with Confectioners' Icing* and sprinkle with Cinnamon Sugar Mixture* and additional raisins, if desired.

* See *Index.*

BOHEMIAN BRAIDED SWEET BREAD

Plaited double-decker loaf.

1 recipe Basic Sweet Dough* made up according to directions, except, before the second addition of flour, add:
2 tsp. grated lemon rind
¼ tsp. mace
1 C. raisins
½ C. chopped walnuts

After dough has been given the second raising and the 10-minute rest, divide it into 6 portions. Shape each portion into a 14-inch strand. Braid 3 strands loosely on lightly greased baking sheet. Braid the other 3 strands tightly on top of the first braid. Let rise double. Bake in preheated oven (375°F.) for 50 to 55 minutes. Frost with Confectioners' Icing.* Decorate with candied cherries and pecan halves.

BREAKFAST BREAD

It is perfection when toasted.

BREAD
¼ C. warm water
1 tbsp. dry yeast
1 C. hot milk
¼ C. sugar
¼ C. soft butter
1 tsp. salt
3¾ C. sifted all-purpose flour
2 egg yolks, slightly beaten

* See *Index*.

FILLING

3 tbsp. hot coffee cream
1 C. finely chopped walnuts
⅓ C. sugar
¼ tsp. salt
½ tsp. vanilla
1 tbsp. butter, melted
1 tbsp. bread crumbs
2 egg whites, beaten until stiff

Dissolve yeast in warm water. Mix milk, sugar, butter, and salt. Cool to lukewarm. Add 2 cups flour and beat well. Add yeast, egg yolks, and the remaining flour. Turn dough out onto floured surface. Knead until smooth and elastic. Place dough in greased bowl and lightly grease top. Cover and let rise until doubled. Punch down. Repeat rising. Divide dough in half. Roll each piece into 8- x 14-inch rectangle. Spread half of filling on each piece within 1 inch of overall border. Roll up jelly roll fashion and place in 2 greased loaf pans (9 x 5 x 3 inches each). Cover and let rise to the top of the pans. Bake in preheated oven (375°F.) for approximately 40 minutes. When loaves are done, remove from pans and lay on sides on a rack to cool.

FILLING RECIPE

Mix hot cream, walnuts, sugar, salt, and vanilla. Sauté bread crumbs in butter until golden. Combine with nut mixture. Fold in egg whites. Spread as directed.

BUTTERSCOTCH-PECAN ROLLS

Upsy-daisy caramels.

    1 recipe Basic Sweet Dough* made up into Traditional
        Cinnamon Rolls* variation
    1 C. butter
    1 C. light brown sugar, packed
    2 tbsp. corn syrup
    1 C. chopped pecans

Melt butter. Add sugar, corn syrup, and pecans. Divide mixture into 3 square greased pans (8 x 8 x 2 inches). Place the 1-inch slices of cinnamon rolls on top of mixture. Let rise until double. Bake in preheated oven (375°F.) for 50 to 60 minutes. Immediately turn pan upside down on a large tray.

CANDIED SWEET BREAD

Filled with fruits.

    1½ tbsp. dry yeast
    ¼ C. warm water
    6 tbsp. butter, melted
    ½ tsp. salt
    ½ C. sugar
    ¾ C. orange juice
    1 tsp. orange rind, grated
    ½ tsp. mace
    ½ C. candied chopped fruit
    ½ C. currants
    4 to 4½ C. sifted all-purpose flour
    1 egg

* See *Index*.

Salad oil
2 tbsp. butter, melted
2 tbsp. sugar

Dissolve yeast in warm water. In mixing bowl, combine
6 tablespoons melted butter, salt, ½ cup sugar, orange
juice, rind, mace, candied fruit, currants, and 3 cups flour.
Beat 4 minutes. Add yeast and egg. Beat in enough additional flour with a wooden spoon so that the dough is
sticky. Knead 3 minutes. Place in a greased bowl, and
brush top with salad oil. Let rise until double. Place in
2 greased loaf pans (9 x 5 x 3 inches). Brush with 2
tablespoons melted butter and sprinkle sugar on top. Let
rise until double. Bake in preheated oven (350°F.) for
35 to 40 minutes.

CURRANT-SPICE ROLLS

The method is so different.

¼ C. butter
3 tbsp. sugar
1 tsp. salt
⅓ C. dried milk
1 egg
2 tbsp. dry yeast
2 C. warm water
5½ to 6 C. sifted all-purpose flour
1 tsp. cinnamon
¼ tsp. nutmeg
1 C. currants

Cream butter, sugar, salt, and dried milk. Beat in egg.
Dissolve yeast in ½ cup warm water. Add to creamed
mixture. Beat in 1 cup flour. Add remainder of water and
4 cups flour. Beat until elastic. Add spices and currants.

Beat in enough additional flour to make a soft dough. Knead 5 minutes. Place in greased bowl. Grease top with butter. Let rise until double. Punch down. Repeat rising. Make up into rolls and place in 2 greased pans (13 x 9 x 2 inches). Let rise until double. Bake in preheated oven (350°F.) approximately 30 to 40 minutes.

DANISH TWIST

A Copenhagen breakfast pretzel.

    1 recipe Basic Sweet Dough*
    ½ C. light raisins
    ½ C. dark raisins
    1 egg yolk
    Confectioners' sugar

Knead raisins into sweet dough. After dough has risen twice, roll it into a slender roll about 24 inches long. Starting at center of roll, twist halves in opposite directions. Lift to lightly greased cookie sheet. Shape into large pretzel shape so ends are barely touching. Brush with beaten egg yolk. Sprinkle with confectioners' sugar and let rise until double in bulk. Bake in preheated (350°F.) for approximately 30 to 40 minutes. Cool on rack. Sprinkle with additional confectioners' sugar.

DILLY ROLLS

Put your herb garden to practical use!

    2 tbsp. dry yeast
    ¼ C. warm water
    2 C. hot milk

* See *Index.*

3 tbsp. sugar
1 tbsp. salt
1 tbsp. dill seed
¼ C. butter
2 eggs
6½ to 7 C. all-purpose flour

Dissolve yeast in warm water, and stir until dissolved. In a large mixing bowl combine hot milk, sugar, salt, dill seed, and butter. When lukewarm, add yeast, eggs, and 3 cups flour. Beat well. With spoon beat in enough flour to make batter smooth and elastic. Turn out on floured board and knead for 5 minutes. Put dough in greased bowl. Grease top and cover with clean towel. Let rise in warm place until doubled in bulk. Punch down and let rise again until doubled. Turn out onto lightly floured board. Shape into 1-inch balls, and place in 2 greased pans (9 x 9 x 2 inches). Brush with slightly beaten egg whites, and sprinkle with additional dill seeds. Let rise half again as much. Bake in preheated oven (450°F.) for 15 to 18 minutes. *Makes 4 dozen.*

EGG YOLK BREAD

Blond and braided.

2 C. milk, warmed
⅓ C. dry yeast
½ tsp. yellow food coloring
½ C. egg yolks
¼ C. sugar
¼ C. salad oil
1½ tsp. salt
7 to 8 C. sifted all-purpose flour

Dissolve yeast in warm milk. Add food coloring. Beat in remaining ingredients. Knead 5 minutes. Grease top. Cover and let rise until double. Punch down and shape in a large braided loaf. Brush with egg yolk glaze. Let rise on a greased baking sheet until almost double. Bake in preheated oven (375°F.) for 45 to 55 minutes.

GRANDMA'S OATMEAL BREAD

Good with a boiled dinner.

2 C. boiling water
2 C. rolled oats
1 tbsp. salt
1 tbsp. butter
1 tbsp. yeast
1 tsp. sugar
¾ C. warm water
⅓ C. brown sugar
4 to 4½ C. sifted all-purpose flour

Add boiling water to rolled oats, salt, and butter. Cool to lukewarm. Dissolve yeast and sugar in ¼ cup warm water, and add to oatmeal mixture. Stir in brown sugar that has been dissolved in ½ cup warm water. Beat in enough flour so that the dough is not sticky. Knead 3 minutes. Place in greased bowl and brush top with butter. Let rise until double. Punch down and divide into 2 parts. Shape, and place in 2 greased pans (9 x 5 x 3 inches). Let rise until double, or to brim of pan. Bake in preheated oven (425°F.) for 15 minutes; reduce heat to 375°F. and finish baking, approximately 30 minutes. When loaves are taken from the oven, they may be brushed with butter for a more tender crust.

HARD-CRUSTED BREAD

When the hens aren't laying.

1½ tsp. dry yeast
2⅔ C. warm water
1 tbsp. salt
1 tbsp. sugar
7½ to 8 C. sifted all-purpose flour
¼ C. yellow corn meal
1 egg white, beaten until frothy

Dissolve yeast in ⅔ cup warm water. Add salt, sugar, and the remaining water. Beat in 5 cups flour until smooth and elastic. Stir in additional flour to make a soft dough. Knead 5 minutes. Place in lightly greased bowl and brush top with salad oil. Let rise in warm place until double. Punch down and let rest 10 minutes. Shape into an oblong. Place seam side down on greased baking sheet that has been sprinkled with corn meal. Brush top with egg white. Let rise in warm place until double. Bake in preheated oven (400°F.) for approximately 50 minutes. *Makes 1 loaf.*

HOLIDAY BREAD

Delicate, fruity bread rising above tops of cans in mosque-like shapes.

1 Basic Sweet Dough* recipe, except, before second
    addition of flour, add
  1 C. raisins
  ½ C. almonds, blanched and chopped
  1 tsp. vanilla

After dough rises, divide it into 3 portions. Place in well-greased 1-pound coffee cans, filling ½ full. Let rise until it puffs over top of can. Bake in preheated oven (375°F.) on low rack for 40 to 45 minutes. Cool 10 minutes. Remove from cans. Spoon Confectioners' Icing* over top, allowing it to drizzle down sides. Sprinkle with multicolored candies.

ICEBOX POTATO ROLLS

Fresh buns every day.

    1 tbsp. dry yeast
    1½ C. warm water
    ⅔ C. soft margarine
    ¾ C. sugar
    1 tbsp. salt
    6 to 6½ C. sifted all-purpose flour
    2 eggs, slightly beaten
    1 C. warm unseasoned mashed potatoes (instant may
      be used)

Dissolve yeast in ½ cup warm water. To large mixing bowl add remainder of water, margarine, sugar, salt, and 3 cups flour. Mix thoroughly. Add yeast, eggs, and mashed potatoes. Beat well. Add enough additional flour to make a dough that is soft. Knead 5 minutes. Place dough in greased bowl and brush top with butter. Cover and keep in refrigerator until ready to be made up. Will keep about 5 days. Form into desired shapes. Let rise until double. Bake in preheated oven (375°F.) for 25 to 30 minutes.

* See *Index*.

J. K.'S SOURDOUGH ROLLS

Like the Conestoga days.

½ C. Sourdough Starter*
1 C. milk
2½ C. sifted all-purpose flour
1 tbsp. sugar
1 tsp. salt
1½ tsp. baking powder
½ tsp. soda
3 tbsp. soft butter, melted

Put starter and milk into bowl with 1 cup flour. Blend together and let stand overnight at room temperature. Sift remaining dry ingredients and beat into dough until all flour is moistened. Knead 1 minute. Shape into rolls and lay in greased pan (8 x 8 x 2 inches). Brush with butter. Let rise 30 minutes in a warm place. Bake in pre-heated oven (400°F.) for 25 to 35 minutes. *Makes 1½ dozen.* Dust with flour.

JULIA'S RAISED DUMPLINGS

To glorify chicken fricassee.

1 tbsp. dry yeast
⅓ C. warm water
1 C. warm milk
2 tsp. salt
1 tbsp. sugar
2 eggs, beaten slightly
2 tsp. dried parsley
4 C. sifted all-purpose flour
1 C. fresh white bread, cut in ½-inch cubes

* See *Index.*

Dissolve yeast in the warm water. Stir in milk, salt, sugar, and eggs. Add parsley and flour. Beat well. Mix in cubed bread. Knead gently for 2 minutes. Put into greased bowl. Lightly grease top. Let rise until double and punch down. Divide dough into 2 pieces. Roll each into a 9-inch oblong. Let rise 10 minutes. Drop into boiling water. Cover with high lid. Boil 12 minutes. Take out and let cool 5 minutes on a towel. Cut into ¾-inch slices with a heavy thread. Let cool completely and put into plastic bag. Reheat by steaming. May be frozen. *Makes 16 pieces.*

MOLASSES OATMEAL BREAD

Sweet; warp-and-woof texture.

2 tbsp. dry yeast
½ C. warm water
1½ C. boiling water
1 C. quick cooking rolled oats
½ C. molasses
⅓ C. shortening
1 tbsp. salt
5½ to 6 C. sifted all-purpose flour
2 eggs, beaten
2 tbsp. oatmeal

Soften yeast in warm water. Pour boiling water into mixing bowl. Add rolled oats, molasses, shortening, and salt. Cool to lukewarm. Beat in two cups flour and eggs. Add yeast. Beat in remaining flour to make a soft dough. The dough will be sticky. Grease top lightly and cover. Place in refrigerator for 2 hours, or leave overnight. Divide dough into 2 pieces on an unfloured board. Shape and place in greased loaf pans (9 x 5 x 3 inches). Let rise in warm place until the dough rises to rim of the pan.

Brush with Egg Yolk Glaze* and sprinkle with 2 table-spoons oatmeal. Bake in preheated oven (375°F.) for 40 to 50 minutes. Do not grease top after it has come out of the oven. *Makes 2 loaves.*

MOM'S BUTTER BREAD

Give us this day our daily . . .

1 C. milk, scalded
3 tbsp. sugar
1 tbsp. salt
6 tbsp. butter
¾ C. tap water
About 6 C. sifted all-purpose flour
1 tbsp. dry yeast, softened in ¼ C. warm water
1 egg

Combine milk, sugar, salt, and butter in mixing bowl, and stir. Add tap water. Beat in 4 cups flour. Add yeast and egg. Beat until elastic. Add enough additional flour to make a dough which is soft, but does not stick to the hands. Knead 3 minutes. Place in greased bowl and brush top lightly with butter. Let rise until double. Punch down and let rise a second time. Put dough on board. Let rest 10 minutes. Divide into two loaves and place in greased bread pans (9 x 5 x 3 inches). Let rise until dough comes even to the top of the pan. Bake in preheated oven (400°F.) about 50 minutes. Remove bread from pan and set on its side on a rack away from drafts. *Makes 2 loaves.*

* See *Index.*

SOUR DOUGH STARTER

The beginning of many good things to eat.

    2 tbsp. dry yeast
    ¾ C. warm water
    4 tsp. sugar
    1½ tsp. salt
    3 C. hot water
    3 C. sifted all-purpose flour

Dissolve yeast in warm water. Stir sugar and salt into hot water until dissolved. Add yeast to mixture. Beat in flour until smooth. Cover and let stand at room temperature 5 days, stirring twice a day. Then store in refrigerator in airtight container. Never use more than 2 cups of starter in a recipe. To replenish starter, add 2 cups warm water and 2 cups sifted all-purpose flour. Beat until smooth.

SPANISH PEASANT BREAD

A jug and a loaf from Pamplona.

    1½ tsp. dry yeast
    ⅔ C. warm water
    1 tbsp. salt
    1 tbsp. sugar

2 C. warm water
8 C. sifted all-purpose flour
¼ C. yellow cornmeal

Dissolve yeast in ⅔ cup water. Combine with salt, sugar, 2 cups water and 5 cups flour. Beat 5 minutes. Add enough remaining flour, beating with wooden spoon, until dough is soft. Knead vigorously for 5 minutes. Place in a large greased bowl and brush top with melted butter. Cover and allow to rise until double. Punch down. Form into 1 large or 2 small oblong rolls. Place on lightly greased baking sheet that has been sprinkled with cornmeal. Brush with Egg Yolk Glaze* and sprinkle with poppy or sesame seeds. Put bread in cold oven and turn oven temperature to 400°F. Bake for 45 to 50 minutes. The bread will rise with the temperature.

SUGAR AND SPICE ROLLS

Nutmeg flavor.

1 recipe Basic Sweet Dough*
½ tsp. nutmeg
Butter, melted
Cinnamon-Sugar Mixture*

Add ½ teaspoon nutmeg to hot milk. Make up rolls, according to method for Basic Sweet Dough. Shape into balls, filling greased muffin pans ½ full. Let rise until double. Bake in preheated oven (400°F.) for approximately 20 minutes. While hot, dip in melted butter and roll in Cinnamon-Sugar Mixture. Place on rack to cool.

* See *Index*.

TRADITIONAL CINNAMON ROLLS

For dinner roll baskets, too.

  1 recipe Basic Sweet Dough* made up according to
      directions
  ½ C. soft butter
  1 C. Cinnamon-Sugar Mixture*

Roll dough to ¼-inch thick. Spread with soft butter
and sprinkle with cinnamon-sugar mixture. Roll up tightly
and cut in 1-inch slices. Place in a greased pan (13 x 9 x
2 inches). Let rise until double. Bake in preheated oven
(375°F.) 55 to 60 minutes. While warm, dribble with
Confectioners' Icing.* Variation: Add ½ cup finely
chopped nuts to Cinnamon-Sugar Mixture and sprinkle
½ cup nuts over icing.

WATER ROLLS

Pile them in a rough-hewn salad bowl.

  1 tbsp. dry yeast
  1 C. warm water
  1 tbsp. sugar
  1 tbsp. salt
  2 tbsp. butter, melted
  3½ to 4 C. sifted all-purpose flour
  2 egg whites, beaten
  Soft shortening
  1 recipe Egg Yolk Glaze*

Dissolve yeast in ½ cup warm water. Add sugar, salt,
and butter to remaining water. Beat in 1 cup flour. Add

* See *Index*.

yeast, egg whites, and 1 cup flour; beat well. Add sufficient flour to make a soft dough. Knead until smooth and elastic, about 5 minutes. Place in greased bowl and brush top with soft shortening. Cover, and let rise in warm place until double. Punch down and repeat rising. Divide dough into 8 pieces. Roll each to 3- to 4-inch length, tapering ends. Place on greased baking sheet. Brush with Egg Yolk Glaze. Let rise until double. Bake in preheated oven (425°F.) approximately 20 to 25 minutes. *Makes 8.*

Cookies

All children love cookies because of their imaginative and appealing shapes and sizes. A house is not a home unless there is a well-filled cookie jar and there is an I-love-you warmth if that cookie jar is kept filled, because Mother rolls and kneads and bakes devotion into each circle and square.

Mother called ours a cookie crock, and it was within easy reach on a low pantry shelf and never empty. Mother's feelings controlled her baking, and so did the seasons. A wintry day might produce soft brown sugar cookies with a plump raisin in the center. Little sister's hurts brought forth her favorite, sugar-coated molasses moons, and Sunday specials were a variety of small fruit-and-nut drop cookies.

Today the cookie crock is hopefully filled with cookies; it most certainly is with memories. Many years ago our crock vanished, but it still holds a place in my affections; and I have often wondered what became of that treasure that held such childhood delights.

BONBON COOKIES

Fill with a surprise.

BATTER
½ C. soft butter
¾ C. sifted confectioners' sugar
1 tbsp. vanilla
¼ tsp. yellow food coloring
1½ C. sifted all-purpose flour
⅛ tsp. salt

FILLING VARIATION
Cherries
Walnuts
Candy pieces
Chocolate-covered nuts

Cream butter, sugar, vanilla, and food coloring. Add flour and salt and beat thoroughly. If dough is dry, add 1 to 2 tablespoons cream. Wrap level tablespoon of dough around filling variations. Refrigerate 1 hour. Place on ungreased baking sheet. Bake in preheated oven (350°F.) for 12 to 15 minutes. When cool, dip in Shiny Glaze Icing.* *Makes 2 dozen.*

BUTTERSCOTCH FRUIT-NUT BARS

A compote of fruits and nuts tucked 'tween caramel layers.

¾ C. butter
2 C. brown sugar, firmly packed
3 eggs

* See *Index.*

1 tsp. vanilla
4 C. sifted cake flour
½ tsp. salt
1 tsp. soda

Cream butter and sugar. Beat in eggs, vanilla, and ½ of the flour. Sift remaining cake flour with salt and soda, and mix with creamed mixture. Chill 1 hour. Divide dough into 2 parts. Roll each into a rectangle ⅛ inch thick. Spread one sheet of dough with cooled filling. Top with second sheet. Press lightly together with a rolling pin. Cut in bars approximately 1 x 3 inches. Place bars on lightly greased cookie sheet. Bake (350°F.) in preheated oven for approximately 25 minutes. When done, bars are light brown. Cool 5 minutes before removing from sheets. *Makes approximately 4 dozen.*

FILLING

1 C. sugar
2 tbsp. flour
1 C. water
1 C. finely cut up dried fruits
1 C. finely chopped walnuts
2 tbsp. lemon juice

Place ingredients in saucepan: stir over direct heat until well blended and thick. Cool.

CANDY GUMDROPS

Little homemakers can begin with this simple recipe and delight sugar-lovin' daddies.

1 C. soft butter
2 C. brown sugar, packed

2 eggs
3½ C. sifted all-purpose flour
1 tsp. soda
1 tsp. salt
1½ C. cut up gumdrops

Cream butter, sugar, and eggs. Sift dry ingredients and add to mixture; blend well. Mix in gumdrops. Chill 1 hour. Drop from teaspoon 2 inches apart on lightly greased baking sheet. Bake in preheated oven (400°F.) 10 to 12 minutes. *Makes 5 dozen.*

CARMEL COOKIE TARTS

Under the butter pastry—a surprise!

½ C. soft butter
1 C. brown sugar, firmly packed
1 egg
½ tsp. vanilla
2 tbsp. milk
1¾ C. sifted all-purpose flour
¼ tsp. salt
½ tsp. soda
1 egg white, slightly beaten
Jam or semisweet chocolate morsels

Cream butter, sugar, egg, vanilla, and milk. Sift dry ingredients and add to creamed mixture. Roll dough to ⅛ inch thick. Cut with 1½-inch cookie cutter. Brush half the rounds with egg white and place 1 teaspoon jam (or chocolate pieces) in center on rounds. Top with another round and press lightly. Cut cross on top with sharp knife so the filling will show through. Place on ungreased cookie sheet. Bake in preheated oven (400°F.) for 10 to 12 minutes. *Makes 4 dozen.*

CHEWY FUDGE BROWNIES

Jim's favorite.

2 squares unsweetened chocolate (2 oz.)
½ C. butter
2 eggs
1⅔ C. sugar
½ tsp. salt
1 tsp. vanilla
1 C. sifted all-purpose flour
1 C. chopped walnuts

Melt chocolate and butter in double boiler. Cool. Beat eggs, sugar, salt, and vanilla. Add to chocolate mixture. Gradually beat in flour. Stir in nuts. Spread in greased and floured pan (8 x 8 x 2 inches). Bake in preheated oven (375°F.) for approximately 50 to 55 minutes. Cut while hot into 16 pieces. May be iced with chocolate frosting, dusted with confectioners' sugar, or served plain.

CHOCOLATE NUT CHIP

Scio County drop cookies.

1 C. soft butter or margarine
¾ C. sugar
¾ C. brown sugar, firmly packed
2 eggs
1 tsp. vanilla
1 tsp. soda
2¼ C. sifted all-purpose flour
1 tsp. salt
1 C. chopped walnuts
2 C. semisweet chocolate morsels

Cream butter with sugars. Beat in eggs and vanilla. Sift dry ingredients and add to mixture. Stir in chopped walnuts and morsels. Drop from teaspoon onto greased baking sheet. Bake in preheated oven (375°F.) for 10 minutes. *Makes 4 dozen.*

COOKIE'S CRACKLED GINGERSNAPS

Crisp and crunchy—great for freezing.

¾ C. margarine
1 C. sugar
1 egg
¼ C. molasses
1 tbsp. ginger
½ tsp. salt
2 tsp. baking soda
1 tsp. cinnamon
2 C. sifted all-purpose flour

Cream margarine and sugar. Beat in egg and molasses. Sift together dry ingredients and add to creamed mixture. Chill for 1 hour. Roll into 1-inch balls. Dip in granulated sugar. Space 2 inches apart on ungreased baking sheet. Bake in preheated oven (350°F.) for 12 to 15 minutes. When done, the cookies will look fluffy and light. Tops will fall and be crinkly when the air hits them. Do not overbake. *Makes approximately 4 dozen.*

CRUNCHY BUTTER DROPS

From the rich results of Kandy's glass churn.

½ C. butter
¾ C. sifted confectioners' sugar
¼ C. milk

1½ C. sifted all-purpose flour
½ tsp. salt
1 tsp. vanilla

Cream butter and sugar. Add milk and mix. Stir in remaining ingredients. Form into 1-inch balls. Place on ungreased cookie sheet. Flatten with bottom of glass dipped in flour. Bake in preheated oven (375°F.) for 10 to 12 minutes. Variation: One square of melted unsweetened chocolate may be added after the milk. *Makes approximately 2 dozen.*

CHEWY OATMEAL COOKIES

Handed down to Kandy from Priscilla Mullins of long ago.

1 C. brown sugar
1 C. butter
1 tsp. vanilla
1 egg
1 C. sifted all-purpose flour
1 tsp. soda
½ tsp. salt
2 C. quick-cooking oats
Pecan halves

Cream sugar and butter. Add vanilla and egg. Beat well. Sift together flour, soda, and salt. Add to creamed mixture. Add quick-cooking oats and mix well. Drop from tablespoon onto lightly greased baking sheet. Top each cookie with pecan half, if desired. Bake in preheated oven (375°F.) for 8 to 10 minutes. If small tea cookies are desired, drop by teaspoonful. If cookies are stored in a tightly covered container, they will become soft and chewy. *Makes 3 dozen.*

CUT-OUT COOKIE DOUGH

To decorate with colored sugars for holiday use.

    1 C. soft butter
    1 C. sugar
    2 eggs
    1 tsp. vanilla
    3 C. sifted all-purpose flour
    ½ tsp. salt

Cream butter and sugar. Add eggs and vanilla. Beat until fluffy. Mix in flour and salt until well blended. Roll dough on floured board until ⅛ inch thick. Cut and shape as desired. Place on ungreased baking sheet. Bake in preheated oven (350°F.) for approximately 12 to 18 minutes. Variation: Double the recipe, and to one half add 4 squares of melted and cooled semisweet chocolate before adding flour. *Makes 4½ dozen.*

DATE BARS

Hearty bars for a harvest feast.

    ¾ C. shortening
    1½ C. sugar
    1 egg
    3 C. sifted all-purpose flour
    1 tsp. salt
    1 tsp. baking powder
    ½ tsp. soda
    1 C. sour milk
    1 C. chopped walnuts, medium fine
    1 C. chopped dates
    1½ C. confectioners' sugar

Cream shortening and sugar. Add egg and beat. Sift dry ingredients, and add alternately with sour milk to the creamed mixture. Fold in walnuts and dates. Spread in a greased and floured pan (13 x 9 x 2 inches). Bake in a preheated oven (350°F.) for approximately 25 minutes. Cool 10 minutes. Cut into bar shape, 1 x 3 inches. Roll in confectioners' sugar. *Makes 36 bars.*

GINGERBREAD MAN

Stand up for my hand-decorated gingerbread men!

1 egg
1 C. molasses
½ C. shortening
3 C. sifted all-purpose flour
1 tsp. baking powder
½ tsp. baking soda
½ tsp. salt
1 tsp. ginger
1½ tsp. cinnamon
1 tsp. cloves
½ tsp. nutmeg
Currants or raisins for decoration

Beat egg, molasses, and shortening. Sift together the dry ingredients and spices. Add to creamed mixture and mix until blended. Chill 1 hour. Roll out dough ¼ inch thick on lightly floured board. Cut out gingerbread man shapes with cutter. Place on ungreased baking sheet. Decorate with currants or raisins for eyes and buttons. Bake in preheated oven (350°F.) for 15 to 20 minutes. Cool. With Royal Icing* make outline for shoes, belt, collar, and cuffs. *Makes about 2 dozen.*

HALF-MOON CRESCENTS

A loving touch shapes a rich batter.

1 C. butter
½ C. granulated sugar
1 tsp. vanilla
2 C. sifted all-purpose flour
1 tbsp. nutmeg
1⅓ C. chopped walnuts
1½ C. sifted confectioners' sugar

Cream butter, granulated sugar, and vanilla. Stir in flour and nutmeg. Add walnuts and blend well. Mold with fingers into half moons. Place on lightly greased baking sheet. Bake in preheated oven (350°F.) until light brown, approximately 20 minutes. While still hot, roll in confectioners' sugar. *Makes 3 dozen.*

JACKIE'S SWIRL COOKIE

Light and dark.

⅔ C. sugar
½ C. margarine
1 tsp. vanilla
2 eggs, well beaten
1½ C. sifted all-purpose flour

* See *Index.*

½ tsp. baking powder
½ tsp. salt
1 C. chocolate chips, melted and cooled

Cream together the sugar, margarine, and vanilla. Add eggs to creamed mixture. Sift together the flour, baking powder, and salt. Blend in the chocolate to give marble effect. Bake in preheated oven (375°F.) for 12 to 15 minutes. *Makes 2 dozen.*

JAM DROP COOKIES

Take it sweet and simple or dress up with a crown.

1 C. sugar
¾ C. butter
1 egg
2 tbsp. milk
¼ C. pineapple preserves or favorite jam
2¼ C. sifted all-purpose flour
1 tsp. soda
½ tsp. salt

Cream sugar and butter. Beat in egg, milk, and pineapple preserves or jam. Sift dry ingredients and add to creamed mixture. Drop from teaspoon 2 inches apart on ungreased baking sheet. Bake in preheated oven (375°F.) for about 10 minutes or until cookies are delicately brown. Cool 1 to 2 minutes before removing from pan. If desired, top each cookie with a bit of pineapple preserves or jam and a walnut half before baking. *Makes 3 dozen.*

JUMBO SUGAR COOKIES

Big as saucers!

1⅓ C. butter
½ C. sugar
2 eggs
1 tbsp. vanilla
3 tbsp. milk
4 C. sifted all-purpose flour
1 tbsp. baking powder
½ tsp. salt
Muscat raisins

Cream butter, sugar, eggs, and vanilla until light and fluffy. Stir in milk. Add dry ingredients. Blend well. Chill 2 hours. Roll ¼ inch thick on lightly floured surface. Cut with 5-inch cutter (coffee can lid). Place 3 large muscat raisins in center and sprinkle top with sugar. Place cookies about 2 inches apart on lightly greased cookie sheet. Bake in preheated oven (375°F.) for 10 minutes, or until lightly browned. Cool slightly and remove from cookie sheet. *Makes about 5 cookies.*

KNIGHTSBRIDGE GINGER COOKIES

With the bite and dash of many spices.

⅓ C. brown sugar, firmly packed
⅔ C. molasses
½ tsp. ginger
½ tsp. cinnamon
½ tsp. cloves
2¼ tsp. soda
½ C. soft margarine
1 egg
2½ C. sifted all-purpose flour

In a one-quart pan cook sugar, molasses, ginger, cinnamon, and cloves to the boiling point. Remove from heat and add soda (mixture will form and thicken). Add margarine, and stir until melted. Put mixture into mixing bowl. Beat in egg and flour. Chill in refrigerator 1 hour. Roll dough to ⅛ inch thick. Cut with cookie cutter. Place cookies on greased cookie sheet 1 inch apart. Bake in preheated oven (350°F.) for 7 to 9 minutes, or until golden. Remove from cookie sheet and cool. Store in airtight container. *Makes approximately 2½ dozen.*

LUCI'S ANISE COOKIES

The flavor and size of a licorice whip.

4 eggs
1¼ C. sugar
1 C. sifted all-purpose flour
1 tsp. anise seeds

Whip eggs and sugar for 10 minutes. Add flour gradually, then the seeds. Pour into a greased and floured pan (8 x 8 x 2 inches). Bake in a preheated oven (375°F.) for 20 minutes. Unmold while hot and slice into strips ⅓ x 4 inches. Place on baking sheet and brown 5 minutes on each side. *Makes approximately 16 cookies.*

MERRY CHRISTMAS COOKIES

A holiday treat for tree trimmers.

⅓ C. soft shortening
⅓ C. sugar
1 egg
⅔ C. honey
1 tsp. lemon flavoring

2 tbsp. milk
2¾ C. sifted all-purpose flour
1 tsp. soda
1 tsp. salt

Mix thoroughly shortening, sugar, egg, honey, flavoring, and milk. Sift in flour, soda, and salt. Beat well. Chill dough one hour. Roll out dough ¼ inch thick. Cut into desired shapes. Place 1 inch apart on lightly greased baking sheet. Bake in a preheated oven (375° F.) until no imprint remains when cookies are touched lightly with finger, about 12 to 15 minutes. When cool, ice and decorate as desired. *Makes 5 dozen.*

MERRY MACAROONS

Chewy and sweet.

2 eggs
¾ C. sugar
⅓ C. sifted all-purpose flour
¼ tsp. baking powder
⅛ tsp. salt
1 tbsp. soft butter
1 tsp. vanilla
2⅔ C. shredded coconut, packed

Beat eggs until foamy. Slowly add sugar and beat until thickened, about 5 minutes. Sift in dry ingredients. Beat in butter, vanilla, and coconut. Drop from teaspoon onto foil-lined sheets. Bake in a preheated oven (325° F.) until browned around edges, about 15 minutes. Cool a few seconds before removing from baking sheets. For Christmas decorations: Before baking, put citron leaves and glacéed cherry halves on top. *Makes 2½ dozen.*

MOLASSES-CHOCOLATE ROLLED COOKIES

A tasty and different combination.

    1 C. butter
    1 C. molasses
    2 C. light brown sugar, packed
    4 C. all-purpose flour
    1 tsp. soda
    ½ tsp. cinnamon
    ½ tsp. salt
    2 sq. grated chocolate
    Frosting and decorations

Cream butter, molasses, and brown sugar until light colored. Sift dry ingredients and spices. Add to batter. Stir in chocolate. Chill dough in refrigerator for several hours. Roll out very thin on lightly floured board. Cut in fancy shapes. Place on greased baking sheet. Bake in preheated oven (350° F.) for 10 to 12 minutes. Cool. Ice with Confectioners' Icing.* Decorate with colored shot, sugar-coated fruits or nuts, gumdrops, and hard candies to produce jewellike effect. *Makes 2½ dozen.*

PINK MERINGUE KISSES

Mom made these for her birthday girls.

    4 egg whites
    ¼ tsp. salt
    1 C. sugar
    1 tsp. maraschino cherry juice
    ¾ C. chopped walnuts, medium fine
    ¼ C. red coloring

* See *Index.*

Beat egg whites with salt until stiff enough to form peaks, but not dry. Gradually beat in sugar, a tablespoon at a time. Stir in maraschino cherry juice, nuts, and food coloring. Drop meringue batter from a teaspoon onto a lightly greased baking sheet, one inch apart. Bake in preheated oven (250° F.) for about one hour. *Makes 4 dozen kisses.*

PEANUT BUTTER BANANA COOKIES

A lunchbox favorite.

½ C. soft shortening
½ C. peanut butter
½ C. granulated sugar
½ C. brown sugar, firmly packed
¼ C. mashed ripe bananas
1¼ C. sifted all-purpose flour
½ tsp. baking powder
¾ tsp. soda
¼ tsp. salt

Cream shortening, peanut butter, and sugars. Add banana and mix. Sift dry ingredients and add to creamed mixture. Chill for 1 hour. Shape in roll. Wrap in wax paper. Chill again 2 hours or overnight. Slice dough into rounds ⅛ to ¼ inch thick. Place on ungreased baking sheet. Bake in preheated oven (350° F.) for 10 minutes. *Makes 3 dozen.*

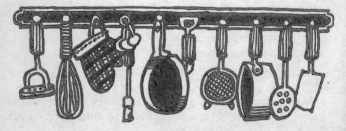

PEANUT BUTTER OATMEAL COOKIES

A down East delight.

¾ C. butter
1¼ C. brown sugar, firmly packed
2 eggs
1 tsp. vanilla
¼ C. peanut butter
2½ C. sifted all-purpose flour
1 tsp. salt
¼ tsp. soda
2 C. quick-cooking oats

Cream butter and brown sugar. Add eggs, vanilla, and peanut butter. Beat until smooth and fluffy. Sift together, flour, salt, and soda, and add to creamed mixture. Fold in oatmeal. Shape into balls and flatten. Place 2 inches apart on lightly greased cookie sheet. Bake in preheated oven (350° F.) for 15 to 18 minutes. *Makes 4 dozen.*

PENNY MISSION COOKIES

Stack high on the trestle table at the church bazaar.

⅔ C. soft butter
1 tsp. vanilla
1⅔ C. sifted all-purpose flour
3 tbsp. light cream
¾ C. chopped walnuts, medium fine
⅔ C. melted butter
1 C. confectioners' sugar

Cream butter, vanilla, and flour. Mix in cream and walnuts. Shape in 1-inch balls. Place on ungreased cookie sheet. Bake in preheated oven (400° F.) approximately 12 to 15 minutes. Cool 3 minutes. Dip in melted butter, and roll in confectioners' sugar. Store overnight before serving. *Makes 2 dozen.*

PETTICOAT COOKIES

Roll over a clean broomstick.

¼ C. butter
½ C. light corn syrup
¼ C. margarine
⅔ C. brown sugar, firmly packed
1 C. sifted all-purpose flour
1 C. chopped pecans

Bring butter, corn syrup, and margarine to a boil. Stir in sugar. Remove from heat. Mix in flour and nuts. Beat until smooth. Drop by rounded teaspoon onto greased baking sheet, 3 inches apart. Bake in preheated oven (350° F.) for 7 to 10 minutes. Cool 1 minute. Remove with spatula. Roll over broomstick while still warm. Replace in oven for a few seconds if they harden before you get to roll them. Cool. *Makes about 1½ dozen.*

POCKET COOKIES

Tiny pouches filled and tucked.

DOUGH
1 C. cream cheese (8 oz.)
1 C. soft butter
2 C. sifted all-purpose flour
¼ tsp. salt
1 egg white, beaten

CUSTARD FILLING

½ tsp. custard flavoring
1 egg yolk
4 tsp. sugar
½ lb. dry cottage cheese
1 tbsp. butter
¼ tsp. salt

Beat cream cheese and butter together until smooth. Mix in flour and salt. For easier rolling, use part of the dough at a time. Roll out dough to approximately ⅛ inch thick. Cut into 2-inch squares. Mix filling ingredients all together. Place approximately ¾ teaspoon of filling on each square. Dot corners with beaten egg white and bring points together to enclose filling. Pinch well to prevent opening. Place pastries on foil paper. Bake in preheated oven (375° F) for about 10 minutes, or until done. May also be made into rounds and cut with cookie cutter, filled, and baked. Variation: Jam, jelly, or commercial fillings may be substituted for custard filling. *Makes 3 dozen.*

RAISIN ROCKS

Good cookies make good neighbors.

2 C. margarine
2 C. brown sugar, firmly packed
2 eggs
3 C. sifted all-purpose flour
½ tsp. salt
2 tsp. soda
½ tsp. cloves
½ tsp. cinnamon
1 C. sour milk
1 C. chopped nuts
1 C. raisins

Cream margarine and sugar. Beat in eggs. Combine dry ingredients. Add alternately with sour milk and mix well. Fold in nuts and raisins. Drop from a teaspoon 2 inches apart on a greased cookie sheet. Bake in preheated oven (350° F.) until light brown, 12 to 15 minutes. *Makes 2½ dozen.*

ROLLED OAT DROP COOKIES

A calico blend of fruits and spices.

½ C. soft butter
1 C. sugar
1 egg
1 tsp. vanilla
5 tbsp. milk
1½ C. sifted cake flour
½ tsp. salt
1 tsp. baking powder
½ tsp. allspice
¾ tsp. cinnamon
½ C. cut up dried fruit
½ C. chopped walnuts
1¾ C. rolled quick-cooking oats

Cream butter and sugar. Beat in egg and vanilla. Add milk. Stir in dry ingredients. Add fruit, walnuts, and rolled oats. Beat well. Drop from teaspoon onto lightly greased cookie sheet. Bake in preheated oven (375° F.) for 10 to 15 minutes. *Makes 2½ dozen.*

ROLLED OATMEAL COOKIES

Wrap in a checkered napkin and take to the creek for
picnics.

¾ C. butter
¾ C. brown sugar, firmly packed
½ C. granulated sugar
2 eggs
1 tsp. vanilla
2½ C. sifted all-purpose flour
¼ tsp. soda
1 tsp. salt
2 C. rolled, quick-cooking oats

Cream butter and sugars. Add eggs and vanilla. Beat
well. Add dry ingredients, beating until smooth. Fold in
oats. Roll dough to less than ¼ inch thick. Cut with
round 2-inch cutter. Place on lightly greased baking
sheet. Bake in preheated oven (350° F.) for 12 minutes.
Cool and decorate, if desired. *Makes 4 dozen.*

SAND TARTS

Remember our mud cookies?

½ C. margarine
1 C. sugar
2 eggs, separated
1 tsp. milk
½ tsp. vanilla
½ tsp. salt
1 tsp. baking powder
1½ C. sifted all-purpose flour
Cinnamon-Sugar Mixture*

* See *Index.*

Cream margarine and sugar. Add yolks, milk, and flavoring. Mix dry ingredients. Add to above and beat. Chill 1 hour. Roll dough very thin. Cut with 2-inch cutter. Put on greased cookie sheet and brush with slightly beaten egg whites. Sprinkle with sugar and cinnamon mixture. Bake in preheated oven (375° F.) for about 8 minutes, or until dark golden color. *Makes 4 dozen.*

SOFT BROWN SUGAR COOKIES

I remember Mama.

    2 C. brown sugar, firmly packed
    1 C. soft shortening
    2 eggs
    ½ C. buttermilk
    ½ tsp. nutmeg
    ½ tsp. salt
    1 tsp. soda
    2 tsp. baking powder
    3½ C. sifted all-purpose flour

Cream sugar and shortening. Stir in eggs and buttermilk. Sift dry ingredients and add to creamed mixture. Chill dough in refrigerator for 1 hour. Roll dough to ¼ inch thick. Cut with 2-inch round cutter. Place on lightly greased baking sheet. Sprinkle with additional sugar. Bake in preheated oven (375° F.) for 10 minutes. Variation: Substitute ½ teaspoon vanilla for nutmeg if cookies are to be frosted. *Makes approximately 3 dozen.*

SOUR CREAM DATE DROPS

Farm kitchen company fare.

- ¼ C. butter or margarine
- ¼ tsp. vanilla
- ¾ C. brown sugar, firmly packed
- 1 egg, beaten
- 1¼ C. sifted all-purpose flour
- ¼ tsp. salt
- ¼ tsp. baking powder
- ½ tsp. soda
- ½ C. thick sour cream
- ¼ C. chopped walnuts
- 2½ doz. pitted dates

Cream butter, vanilla, and sugar. Add eggs and beat. Add sifted dry ingredients alternately with sour cream. Stir smooth after each addition. Add nuts. Place dates on lightly greased cookie sheet. Drop small portions of mixture on top of each date. Bake in preheated oven (400° F.) for about 10 minutes. When still warm, spread with Confectioners' Icing.* *Makes 2½ dozen.*

TOASTED SEED WAFERS

A New England herb cracker.

- ¾ C. soft butter
- 2 C. brown sugar, firmly packed
- 2 eggs
- 1 C. sifted all-purpose flour
- ½ tsp. baking powder
- ¼ tsp. salt

* See *Index.*

¼ C. sesame seeds
½ C. chopped walnuts, medium fine
1 tsp. vanilla

Cream butter and sugar. Beat in eggs. Sift flour, baking powder, salt, and add to creamed mixture. Toast sesame seeds in ungreased frying pan over medium heat. Cool. Stir in walnuts, vanilla, and sesame seeds. Drop from teaspoon onto greased and floured cookie sheet. Bake in preheated oven (375° F.) for approximately 10 minutes. Cool 1 minute before removing from sheet. *Makes 4 dozen.*

YUMMY DROPS

All the pantry goodies added to this cookie.

6 egg whites
1 C. sugar
2 C. graham cracker crumbs
1 C. chopped dates
1 C. chopped pecans
¾ C. shredded coconut
½ tsp. vanilla or rum extract

Beat egg whites until stiff. Add sugar and continue beating. Stir in remaining ingredients. Drop from teaspoon onto lightly greased baking sheet. Bake in preheated oven (350° F.) for 10 minutes. Keep in airtight container. *Makes approximately 3 dozen.*

Cakes

When I was growing up, elaborate, decorated cakes had but one meaning—some member of the family had reached another birthday! Each cake was original and, always, unusual. Candles of course were important, but equally so for me was the fun of helping Mother, unless it was July 10, my occasion to be honored.

Birthday cakes were made to be very personal and brought out at dessert time for a "big surprise." This called for box camera snapshots; the happy faces are enshrined today in our scrapbooks.

Mother often mused, "I wish I knew how many cakes I have baked since my first one." Not only on birthdays did we have cake, but almost each night for supper. We were never held down to one piece, and there always seemed to be plenty. For a long time banana whipped cream was our favorite, and nesselrode was a treat, too. Sometimes Mother made applesauce cake without frosting, and this was the best kind for snacks the next day.

Today, even though I have mastered professional cake decorating, I still reminisce at my work, for into each confection goes a memory and the inspiration to achieve my best.

APPLE CAKE

Moist and rich with or without frosting.

½ C. margarine
1½ C. light brown sugar, packed
3 eggs
3 medium tart apples, peeled, cored, and ground
2¼ C. sifted cake flour
¾ tsp. salt
½ tsp. cloves
1½ tsp. cinnamon
1 tsp. soda
1½ C. buttermilk

Cream margarine, brown sugar, and eggs until fluffy. Stir in apples. Sift dry ingredients and add alternately with buttermilk to the creamed mixture. Pour into 2 greased and floured cake pans (8 inch). Bake in preheated oven (350° F.) approximately 25 to 30 minutes.

CHOCOLATE FUDGE CAKE

My husband said, "Make it again."

½ C. sugar
1½ tsp. baking soda
1¼ C. Dutch cocoa
6 tbsp. butter
½ C. margarine
½ tsp. salt

Cream all together for 4 minutes. Scrape down sides of bowl and continue for 1 minute.

1¼ C. sugar
1½ C. sifted cake flour
¾ tsp. cream of tartar
1 C. milk, room temperature

Mix all together and add first mixture. Cream 6 minutes.

1 C. eggs
½ C. milk
1 tsp. vanilla

Add to the combined mixtures and blend 4 minutes. Pour batter into 3 greased and floured cake pans (9 inch). Bake in preheated oven (350° F.) for 35 to 45 minutes.

COCOA MERINGUE TORTE

A surprise for company. Elegant and luscious, yet so easy.

1 package yellow cake mix
4 egg whites
⅛ tsp. cream of tartar
Pinch of salt
¾ C. sugar
¾ C. chopped walnuts
1 recipe Cocoa Whipped Cream*

Prepare yellow cake mix according to directions on box. Pour batter into 2 greased and floured pans (8 inch). Beat egg whites until foamy. Add cream of tartar and salt. Continue beating until soft peaks form. Add sugar and beat until dissolved. Fold in nuts. Spread mixture over cake pan batters. Bake in preheated oven (375° F.) for 25 to 30 minutes. Cool in pans for 10 minutes. Remove from pans and finish cooling. Spread Cocoa Whipped Cream between layers and add remaining whipped cream on top. *Serves 10*.

*See *Index*.

CORNSTARCH SPONGE CAKE

Grandma Dexter's Friday night cake.

    6 eggs, separated
    1¼ C. sugar
    2 tbsp. lemon juice
    ½ tsp. salt
    ¾ C. sifted cake flour
    ¼ C. cornstarch

Leave eggs at room temperature for 1 hour. Beat egg whites with salt until stiff. Using same beater, beat yolks, sugar, lemon juice, and salt for 5 minutes. Fold into egg white mixture. Mix flour and cornstarch together. Fold into egg mixture, and mix until there are no more flour streaks. Pour batter into 3 ungreased cake pans (8 inch). Bake in preheated oven (350° F.) for approximately 20 minutes. Invert pans to cool. Run knife along edges and take out. Fill layers with favorite filling. Frost with icing or serve with whipped cream and strawberries. *Serves 10 to 12*.

DOUBLE DECKER PECAN FUDGE CAKE

I like this one, too.

    ¾ C. butter
    2¼ C. sugar
    3 eggs

3 oz. unsweetened chocolate, melted and cooled
1½ tsp. vanilla
3 C. sifted cake flour
1½ tsp. baking soda
¾ tsp. salt
1½ C. ice water
1 C. chopped pecans

Cream butter and sugar. Add eggs one at a time, beating well after each addition. Stir in melted chocolate and vanilla. Combine dry ingredients. Mix into egg mixture alternately with ice water. Beat smooth. Fold in pecans. Pour batter into 2 greased and floured pans (9 inch). Bake in preheated oven (375° F.) for approximately 30 to 35 minutes.

EGG YOLK SPONGE CAKE

Rich and yellow.

6 egg yolks
1 C. sugar
½ C. boiling water
2 tsp. vanilla
1 tsp. lemon extract
1½ C. sifted cake flour
2 tsp. baking powder
½ tsp. salt

Beat egg yolks until thick and lemon colored. Add sugar gradually. Blend in slowly at low speed the boiling water and flavorings. Combine dry ingredients. Add to above. Pour batter into 2 greased and floured pans (8 or 9 inch). Bake in preheated oven (350° F.) for 25 to 30 minutes. Cool 15 minutes. Take out of pans. Fill layers and frost as desired.

FLUFFY CHEESE CAKE

A famous airline chef's recipe—a farmer's daughter does travel.

CRUST
1¾ C. finely rolled cornflakes
½ C. sugar
1½ tsp. cinnamon
½ C. soft butter

Mix all ingredients thoroughly. Grease spring form pan (9 x 3 inches). Press mixture onto bottom and ¾ way up the sides of the pan.

BATTER
1 C. sugar
¼ C. sifted all-purpose flour
¼ tsp. salt
2¾ C. cream cheese
1 C. eggs
½ tsp. grated lemon rind
½ tsp. vanilla
3 tbsp. heavy cream

Combine sugar, flour, and salt. Beat cream cheese until smooth, and gradually add sugar mixture. Slowly add eggs, rind, vanilla, and cream. Whip until smooth. Push batter into prepared pan. Bake in preheated oven (400° F.) for 15 minutes. Continue baking for 20 to 25 minutes, at 375° F. *Serves 8 to 10.*

FRESH STRAWBERRY SPONGE CAKE

In early summer I always picked wild berries for this one.

4 eggs, separated
¼ tsp. salt
¾ C. granulated sugar
1 tsp. vanilla
2 tbsp. water
¾ C. sifted cake flour
1 tsp. baking powder
1½ C. heavy cream
6 tbsp. confectioners' sugar
3 C. strawberry halves or the tiny wild ones in the
    berry patch

Beat egg whites with salt until stiff but not dry. Gradually beat in half the sugar, adding about 2 tablespoons at a time. In another bowl beat egg yolks with remaining sugar, vanilla, and water until thick and lemon colored. Gently fold in egg whites. Fold in cake flour and baking powder gradually, about ¼ cup at a time until mixed. Grease and flour pan (12 x 18 x 1 inches). Pour batter into pan and spread evenly. Bake in preheated oven (375° F.) for 12 to 15 minutes. Loosen sides and bottom and remove from pan onto clean linen kitchen towel. Cut off the four crisp edges with a sharp knife. Roll up cake, starting at short end, like a jelly roll. Wrap in towel and cool on cake rack. About 1 hour before serving, whip the cream and confectioners' sugar. Unroll cake. Fill with half the whipped cream and a layer of berries that have been dipped in confectioners' sugar. Roll cake up again and spread outside with remaining whipped cream. Top with sliced strawberries as garnish. *Serves 8 to 10.*

GINGER GEM CUPCAKES

For the box lunch.

½ C. margarine
½ C. sugar
1 egg
¾ C. molasses
2 C. sifted all-purpose flour
1 tsp. baking soda
½ tsp. salt
1 tsp. ginger
1 tsp. cinnamon
1 C. commercial sour cream

Cream margarine and sugar. Beat in egg and molasses. Blend dry ingredients and spices. Add this to cream mixture alternately with sour cream. Line muffin tins with crinkle cups and fill ⅔ full. Bake in preheated oven (350° F.) for 20 to 25 minutes. *Makes 2 dozen.*

Serve plain or with Seafoam Frosting.*

GINGERY BREAD CAKE

Try it with warm lemon sauce.

½ C. butter
¼ C. margarine
½ C. sugar
1 egg
1 C. buttermilk
1 C. molasses
1 C. sifted cake flour
¾ C. sifted all-purpose flour
1½ tsp. baking soda

* See *Index*

¼ tsp. salt
1 tsp. ginger
1 tsp. cinnamon
½ tsp. cloves

Cream butter, margarine, and sugar. Mix in egg, butter-milk, and molasses. Combine dry ingredients. Stir into batter until flour is blended. Pour into greased and floured loaf pan (13 x 9 x 2 inches). Bake in preheated oven (375° F.) for 30 minutes or until done. Cool in pan. *Serves 10 to 12.*

GOLD CAKE

A sunshine delight.

¾ C. butter
1½ C. sugar
6 egg yolks
3 C. sifted cake flour
2 tsp. baking powder
¼ tsp. salt
¼ tsp. mace
2 tbsp. grated orange rind
1 C. lukewarm milk

Cream butter and sugar. Add egg yolks. Beat until light and fluffy. Combine flour, baking powder, salt, mace, and orange rind. Fold into egg mixture alternately with milk. Mix well. Divide mixture into 3 greased and floured layer pans (8 inch), filling them ½ full. Bake in pre-heated oven (325° F.) for 25 minutes. *Serves 10 to 12.*

GRATED ORANGE CHIFFON CAKE

Lacy to look at; tangy to taste.

   2¾ C. sifted cake flour
   1⅔ C. sugar
   1 tbsp. baking powder
   1 tsp. salt
   ⅔ C. salad oil
   6 egg yolks
   ⅔ C. water
   3 tbsp. grated orange rind
   ¾ tsp. cream of tartar
   1¼ C. egg whites

Sift flour, sugar, baking powder, and salt. Make a well and add oil, egg yolks, water, and orange rind. Stir until smooth. Beat egg whites with cream of tartar until stiff peaks are formed. Gradually pour egg yolk mixture over beaten egg whites, folding until blended. Pour into ungreased tube pan (10 x 4 inches). Bake for approximately 60 to 75 minutes at 325° F. Invert over funnel and cool. Put on serving plate, cover with a fancy paper doily, and sift confectioners' sugar over top. Remove doily. *Serves 10 to 12.*

LEMON RIND POUND CAKE

One for you and one for a neighbor.

   8 egg yolks
   1¾ C. butter
   2¼ C. sugar
   3¾ C. sifted cake flour
   1 tsp. baking powder
   1 tsp. nutmeg

1 tsp. salt
1 tsp. grated lemon rind
8 egg whites

Beat yolks until thick and lemon colored. Cream butter
and sugar. Add to yolks. Combine dry ingredients and
lemon rind. Mix with creamed mixture. Whip egg whites
until stiff but not dry. Fold into yolk mixture. Pour into
greased and floured loaf pan (9 x 5 x 2 inches). Bake
in preheated oven (350°F.) for 45 to 50 minutes.

MACAROON ANGEL CAKELETS

Light and feathery.

¾ C. sifted all-purpose flour
½ tsp. baking powder
1⅓ C. sugar
1 C. shredded coconut
6 egg whites
½ tsp. salt
½ tsp. cream of tartar
½ tsp. vanilla
½ tsp. almond extract

Combine flour, baking powder, 1 cup sugar, and coconut. Whip egg whites with salt and cream of tartar until
soft peaks form. Add ⅓ cup sugar and beat stiff. Fold
in flour mixture and flavorings. Mix until blended. Spoon
into muffin tins lined with crinkle cups, filling to within
¼ inch of the brim. Before baking, cakes may be decorated with a sprinkling of colored coconut. Bake in
preheated oven (325° F.) for 55 to 60 minutes. *Makes 16.*

MAPLE CRUNCH CHIFFON CAKE

Soft yet textured—opposites attract.

8 egg whites
¾ tsp. cream of tartar
1½ tsp. salt
2 C. sifted cake flour
¾ C. granulated sugar
¾ C. light brown sugar, packed
1 tbsp. baking powder
½ C. salad oil
6 egg yolks
½ C. cold water
2 tsp. maple flavoring
½ C. finely chopped walnuts

Whip egg whites with cream of tartar and salt, and beat until stiff but not dry. Sift dry ingredients into mixing bowl. Add salad oil, egg yolks, water, and flavoring. Fold egg yolk batter into egg whites. Add nuts. Push batter into ungreased tube pan (10 inch). Bake in preheated oven (325° F.) for approximately 55 to 60 minutes. Invert on funnel and cool. *Serves 12.*

MARTHA'S BOILED SPICE CAKE

From my neighbor on yonder hill. I do miss our back-and-forth treks.

2 C. water
¾ C. margarine
2 tsp. cinnamon
1 tsp. allspice
2 tsp. cloves
1 C. brown sugar, packed

1 C. granulated sugar
¼ C. raisins
¼ C. chopped nuts
2½ C. sifted all-purpose flour
2 tsp. baking soda

Simmer all ingredients except flour and baking soda for 5 minutes. Cool. Blend in flour and baking soda. Pour into greased and floured pan (13 x 9 x 2 inches). Bake in preheated oven (350° F.) for approximately 30 minutes. *Serves 10 to 12 neighbor ladies.*

MY MOM'S ROLL JAM CAKE

Brings back a childhood memory: a red-checkered oil tablecloth, and this for dessert.

4 eggs
1 C. sugar
½ tsp. vanilla
1 C. sifted all-purpose flour
2 tsp. baking powder
1 tsp. salt
Raspberry jam for filling

Cream eggs, sugar, and vanilla. Combine dry ingredients. Add to mixture. Beat until well mixed. Pour batter into greased and floured baking sheet (10 x 15 x 1 inch). Bake in preheated oven (350° F.) for 8 to 10 minutes. Turn warm cake out of pan onto a kitchen towel. Cut crisp edges with sharp knife. Spread all of it with raspberry jam, or your favorite. Roll up in jelly roll fashion. Sift confectioners' sugar on top. *Cut into 8 slices.*

PINEAPPLE UPSIDE DOWN CAKE

I bet my mother's is better than your mother's.

¼ C. butter, melted
½ C. soft light brown sugar, packed
5 pineapple slices
5 cherries
¾ C. chopped pecans
½ C. margarine
¾ C. granulated sugar
2 eggs
¾ C. warmed milk
1 tsp. vanilla
⅔ C. sifted all-purpose flour
2½ tsp. baking powder
½ tsp. salt
20 graham crackers, rolled fine (or 2 C.)

Grease and flour square cake pan (9 x 9 x 2 inches). Mix melted butter and soft brown sugar. Spread on bottom of pan. Place pineapple and cherries in sugar mixture in a decorative pattern. Sprinkle with pecans. Cream margarine and granulated sugar. Beat in eggs. Add milk and vanilla. Combine flour, baking powder, salt, and cracker crumbs. Add to the creamed mixture and stir until well blended. Pour batter into pan. Bake in preheated oven (350° F.) 45 to 50 minutes. Cool 5 minutes. Invert on serving platter. Excellent with whipped cream. *Serves 8.*

POINTERS FOR FRUIT CAKE

Read this before Thanksgiving.

Fruit cakes rise very little, as a rule, so fill pans nearly full. Cool before turning out of pans. Store, wrapped in aluminum foil, in a cool place. Chill before slicing. Make fruit cake 1 month before it is to be eaten. Only dark fruit cakes ripen well. White fruit cakes will keep approximately 1 month. Fruit cakes freeze very well. To ripen fruit cakes: (1) Pour a small amount of brandy over cake; (2) wrap in cheesecloth. Repeat brandy treatment every day for 7 days. Before using, glaze with warm corn syrup. Let stand for 30 minutes, and decorate with candied fruits and nuts.

POPPY SEED CAKE

Old world favorite.

- ⅔ C. poppy seed
- ½ C. warmed milk
- ¾ C. butter
- 1½ C. sugar
- 1 tsp. vanilla
- 2¾ C. sifted all-purpose flour
- 4 tsp. baking powder
- 1 C. milk
- 4 egg whites, beaten

Soak poppy seed in warmed milk for 2 hours. Cream butter, sugar, and vanilla. Combine flour and baking powder. Add to creamed mixture alternately with milk. Add poppy seed. Fold in beaten egg whites. Pour batter into greased and floured Turk's head form pan (9 x 3½ inches). Bake in preheated oven (350° F.) for 30 to 35 minutes. Cool 10 minutes. Remove from pan. Frost when cold with Cinnamon Dribble Glaze* *Serves 10 to 12*.

POPPY SEED FORM CAKE

A textured treat.

½ C. whole poppy seed
1 C. milk
¾ C. butter or margarine
1 C. granulated sugar
2½ C. sifted cake flour
2½ tsp. baking powder
1 tsp. vanilla
⅔ C. egg whites
¼ C. granulated sugar

Soak poppy seeds in milk for 30 minutes. Cream butter well. Add 1 cup sugar a little at a time. Beat until light and creamy but not runny. Sift flour and baking powder together. Add flour to creamed mixture alternately with milk and poppy seed mixture. Add vanilla. Beat egg whites until they cling to bowl. Add ¼ cup sugar and beat until blended, but not dry. Fold beaten egg whites into batter until no streaks can be seen. Pour into Turk's head form pan (9 x 3½ inches) that has been well greased and floured. Bake in preheated oven (325° F.) for 45 minutes; raise heat to 375° F. and bake for about 15 minutes more, or until cake is done when tested. Cool in pan about 10 minutes. Loosen around top and tube and invert onto cake cooler. When cool, drizzle with Cinnamon Dribble Glaze* or Lemon Butter Icing.*

* See *Index.*

POPPY SEED POUND CAKE

This one is good too.

5 egg whites
1 C. butter
1 C. sugar
1 tsp. vanilla extract
1 tsp. lemon extract
5 egg yolks
¼ C. poppy seed
1 C. sifted all-purpose flour
1 tsp. baking powder

Beat egg whites and set aside. Without cleaning the beaters, cream butter, sugar, and flavorings until light. Add yolks and poppy seed and continue to beat until blended. Combine flour and baking powder. Sprinkle flour mixture over beaten egg whites and fold gently until there are no more streaks left. Stir egg white mixture into the yolk mixture until it is well mixed. Pour batter into greased and floured loaf pan (9 x 5 x 3 inches). Bake in preheated oven (375° F.) for approximately 1 hour. May be frosted with Cinnamon Dribble Glaze.* *Serves 8 to 10.*

PRUNE AND NUT CAKE

Reminiscent of my farm days.

½ C. butter
1½ C. sugar
2 eggs, beaten
1 C. coarsely cut and seeded prunes
2½ C. sifted cake flour

* See *Index.*

¾ tsp. baking powder
1 tsp. baking soda
½ tsp. salt
1 tsp. cloves
1 tsp. allspice
1 tsp. cinnamon
1 C. buttermilk
½ C. chopped pecans

Cream butter and sugar. Add eggs and prunes. Combine all dry ingredients. Add flour mixture alternately with buttermilk. Mix well. Stir in nuts. Pour into 2 greased and floured layer pans (9 inch). Bake in preheated oven (375° F.) for 35 to 40 minutes. Cool. Frost as desired. *Serves 10.*

SPANISH BRANDY CHEESE CAKE

For candlelight and roses.

1⅓ C. sifted confectioners' sugar
¼ C. brandy
2 C. cream cheese, room temperature
1 tsp. unflavored gelatin
½ C. cold water
2 C. heavy cream, whipped
1 graham cracker pie shell (8 or 9 inch)

Whip sugar, brandy, and cream cheese until blended. Soften gelatin in cold water. Melt over hot water. Add gelatin to the cream cheese mixture, and continue to whip. Fold in whipped cream. Pour into pie shell. Chill until firm. *Serves 8.*

SPICE CAKE

Don't use a beater!

2¼ C. sifted cake flour
1 tsp. baking powder
¾ tsp. baking soda
1 tsp. salt
¾ tsp. cloves
¾ tsp. cinnamon
⅛ tsp. black pepper
¾ C. shortening, butter, or margarine
¾ C. brown sugar, packed
1 C. granulated sugar
1 tsp. vanilla
3 eggs
1 C. buttermilk or sour milk

Sift flour, baking powder, baking soda, salt, cloves, cinnamon, and pepper. With your hands work or cream the shortening, butter, or margarine with a beating motion until it looks like whipped cream. If brown sugar is lumpy, sift or roll it. Begin to work the brown sugar in gradually. Work the granulated sugar in gradually. Add vanilla. Continue creaming until mixture is very fluffy and the grains of sugar almost disappear (this is the trick that makes a wonderful texture). Add eggs one at a time, beating hard after each addition. Stir in the flour mixture alternately with the buttermilk. Pour batter into 3 greased pans (8 inch). Bake in preheated oven (350° F.) for 30 to 35 minutes. Cool in pan 5 minutes. Turn out on cake rack and cool completely. *Serves 12.*

WHITE ANGEL CAKE

High and light in the olden way.

    1¾ C. egg whites (about 13)
    1⅔ C. sugar (superfine granulated)
    1¼ C. sifted cake flour
    ½ tsp. salt
    2 tbsp. water
    1½ tsp. lemon juice
    1¼ tsp. cream of tartar
    ¾ tsp. vanilla
    ½ tsp. almond extract

Allow egg whites to stand at room temperature for 1 hour. Sift the sugar. Add to the flour ½ cup sifted sugar and the salt. Beat egg whites with the water and lemon juice until mixture is foamy. Add cream of tartar and resume beating. It is important to stop beating the mixture when it is stiff enough to stand alone yet still has a moist, shiny appearance. Gradually and gently whip the remaining sugar into egg whites, about 2 tablespoons at a time. Fold in vanilla and almond extracts. Fold in gradually the sifted flour and sugar mixture, about 1 tablespoon at a time. Use a gentle folding motion until the sugar and flour are well blended with the egg whites. If overmixed, the grain will be coarse. Push the batter into an ungreased tube pan (10 x 4 inches). Gently cut through the batter. Bake in preheated oven (325° F.) for about 1 hour and 15 minutes. Cake is done when crust is a delicate brown and does not retain an imprint when touched lightly. Invert pan on a funnel and let hang until cake is cold, about 1 hour. Frost as desired. Holiday variations: (1) Tint parts of batter with food colorings. (2) Chocolate Angel Cake is made by substituting ¼ cup cocoa for ¼ cup flour in the recipe. Sift the flour and cocoa together, and proceed as for plain angel cake. *Serves 10 hungry people.*

WHITE ANGEL FOOD CAKE

Heavenly delight.

2 C. egg whites
1⅓ C. sifted cake flour
2 tsp. cream of tartar
¼ tsp. salt
½ tsp. vanilla
2 C. confectioners' sugar
1 C. granulated sugar

Beat egg whites, cream of tartar, salt, and vanilla until foamy. Gradually add granulated sugar until meringue holds stiff peaks. Sift confectioners' sugar and cake flour together. Sprinkle sugar and flour mixture over meringue, folding in gently. Push batter into greased tube pan (10 x 4 inches). Cut through batter. Bake in preheated oven (360° F.) for 60 to 70 minutes. Invert tube pan on funnel. Let hang until cake is completely cool. Frost or leave plain.

WHITE BRIDAL CAKE

For that perfect day.

14-INCH TIER
3 C. soft butter
6 C. sugar
12 C. sifted cake flour
¼ C. baking powder
4 C. lukewarm milk
2 tsp. salt
2 tsp. vanilla
28 egg whites

10- AND 6-INCH TIERS
1½ C. soft butter
3 C. sugar
6 C. sifted cake flour
2 tbsp. baking powder
2 C. lukewarm milk
1 tsp. salt
1 tsp. vanilla
14 egg whites

9-INCH TIER (MAKES 2)
¾ C. soft butter
1½ C. sugar
3 C. sifted cake flour
1 tbsp. baking powder
1 C. lukewarm milk
½ tsp. salt
½ tsp. vanilla
7 egg whites

Cream butter and ½ of the sugar. Combine dry ingredients. Add milk alternately with dry ingredients to creamed mixture. Beat egg whites until soft peaks form. Add sugar gradually. Blend in salt and vanilla. Fold egg whites into batter. Pour into greased and floured pans, filling ⅔ full. Bake in preheated oven until done. Slow baking gives cake fine texture.

Approximate baking time:
14-inch tier: 30 minutes at 350°F., then 1½ hours at 325° F.;
10-inch tier: 25 minutes at 350°F., then 1 to 1½ hours at 325° F.;
9-inch tier: 20 minutes at 350°F., then 15 to 20 minutes at 325° F.;
6-inch tier: 20 minutes at 350°F., then 15 to 20 minutes at 325° F.

WHITE POUND CAKE

Can be sliced and toasted for breakfast.

½ C. butter
1¼ C. sugar
2 C. sifted cake flour
1½ tsp. baking powder
1 tsp. salt
½ C. lukewarm milk
4 egg whites, beaten
1 tsp. vanilla
Confectioners' sugar

Cream butter and sugar. Mix dry ingredients. Add to creamed mixture alternately with milk. Fold in egg whites with vanilla. Pour batter into greased and floured loaf pan (9 x 5 x 3 inches). Bake in preheated oven (350° F.) for approximately 50 minutes. Cool in pan 10 minutes. Remove from pan, dust with confectioners' sugar. *Serves 10.* Variation: Add ½ cup pecan halves on top of batter or ½ cup chopped toasted pieces to batter.

WIND AND WATER CAKE

When the chicks didn't lay for Mom.

1 C. mince meat
1 C. cold water
1 C. sugar
½ C. margarine
½ tsp. cinnamon
¼ tsp. cloves
⅛ tsp. salt
1 tsp. baking soda
2 C. sifted all-purpose flour

Put in saucepan: mince meat, water, sugar, margarine, cinnamon, cloves, and salt. Boil 1 minute. Add soda and flour. Stir. Pour batter into greased and floured pan (9 x 9 inches). Bake in preheated oven (350°F.) for approximately 25 to 30 minutes. *Serves 8.*

YELLOW DAISY CAKE

To brighten a rainy day.

    17 egg whites
    1 tsp. salt
    1 tsp. cream of tartar
    ¾ C. sugar
    10 egg yolks
    1 tsp. vanilla
    1½ C. sifted cake flour
    1⅔ C. sifted confectioners' sugar

Whip egg whites, salt, and cream of tartar until soft peaks form. Beat sugar in gradually. Beat egg yolks until thick and lemon colored. Gently fold egg yolk mixture into whites. Add vanilla. Fold in flour and confectioners' sugar. Push batter into ungreased tube pan (10 inch). Bake in preheated oven (350° F.) for approximately 60 to 70 minutes. Invert over funnel until cold. *Serves 10 to 12.*

Frostings

Auntie Ford, as we called her, used to come to the farmhouse a few times a year for a week at a time and help with the sewing. Each afternoon, after a long session with the old treadle White machine and lengths of dotted swiss or gingham plaids, she would come to the kitchen with pins bristling in her bodice for a cup of tea. Mama would be deep in supper preparations, and if she were frosting a cake, Auntie Ford invariably said, "Company coming?" And each time Mama would patiently say, "This is just for dinner tonight for the family."

It was never too much trouble for Mother to ice a cake—she creamed her weight many times over in butter and sugar and stirred vats of boiled frostings. To her it was as simple a routine as putting on the granite coffee pot to perk or setting the table. Of course, gingerbreads could be glorified with whipped cream or a moist apple cake eaten as is, but every cake was a finished product. We took turns licking the frosting bowl, but Mama always let me finish up her frosted cake with swirls and patterns. Today when I work with spun sugar or butter cream rosettes I think of importantly brandishing the spatula in the kitchen on Norton Summit Road.

ANGEL MERINGUE

Use on cream pies or meringue shells.

½ C. egg whites
1¼ C. sugar
½ C. water

Boil water and sugar to 240°F. Beat whites until stiff. Add boiled sugar gradually while beating. Continue to beat until cool. *Will cover 2 9-inch pies.*

ANGEL WHITE FROSTING

Angel feather goodness.

¼ C. cake flour
¾ C. milk
¾ C. sugar
¾ C. vegetable shortening
1½ tsp. vanilla

Bring milk and flour to boil. Cool. Cream sugar, shortening, and vanilla until it is fluffy. Add milk and flour mixture. Continue beating 3 minutes. *Will frost and fill an 8-inch 2-layer cake.*

BAKED BLACK WALNUT FROSTING

A one-step ice and bake.

3 egg whites
¼ tsp. salt
3 C. brown sugar, firmly packed
⅓ C. chopped black walnuts

Beat egg whites and salt to medium stiffness. Add brown sugar and continue beating until stiff. Fold in nuts. Spread on unbaked spice loaf or layer cake. Bake same as for required cake time. *Will frost one cake (13 x 9 x 2 inches) or 3 layers (8 inches).*

BANANA FLUFF FROSTING

For a lazy day.

1 C. mashed ripe bananas
½ C. sugar
Dash of salt
1 egg white

With electric mixer, combine all ingredients and beat until thick and fluffy, about 8 minutes. *Makes 5 cups, which will cover and fill 8- or 9-inch 3-layer cake.*

BROWN BUTTER ICING

Tried and true.

¼ C. butter
2 C. sifted confectioners' sugar
2 tbsp. coffee cream
1 tsp. salad oil
1½ tsp. vanilla
1 tbsp. hot water, if needed

Melt butter, and keep over low heat until light brown. Blend in sugar and remaining ingredients. If icing is not of spreading consistency, add the hot water and blend. *Will frost 1 loaf cake (13 x 9 x 2 inches).*

BUTTER-CHOCOLATE FILLING

Tuck between layer cakes for yumminess.

3 eggs, beaten
¾ C. sugar
¾ C. semisweet chocolate pieces, melted
¾ C. butter, taken from refrigerator

Mix sugar and eggs. Cook 10 minutes in double boiler, stirring constantly. Add melted chocolate. Mix until smooth. Cool completely. Cream butter. Beat in chocolate mixture until smooth. *Will fill a three-layer cake (8 or 9 inch).*

CARAMEL DIPS

For wee cream puffs.

4½ C. sugar
1 C. water
1 tbsp. corn syrup

Put all ingredients into saucepan. Wash down sides while cooking with brush dipped in water. Cook sugar syrup to 325°F. Remove from heat. Place pan in ice water for 1 minute. Dip filled cream puffs in syrup one at a time with a large fork. Let drip on rack. Serve puffs with a topping of chocolate syrup.

CHOCOLATE CREAM CHEESE FLUFF

½ C. cream cheese
2 eggs
1 tsp. vanilla
¼ tsp. salt
3¾ C. sifted confectioners' sugar
3 squares bitter chocolate (3 oz.), melted and cooled

Cream all ingredients and beat until smooth. *Will frost a 2-layer cake (8 or 9 inch).*

CHOCOLATE ICING

3 C. sifted confectioners' sugar
1 tsp. salt
2 eggs
⅔ C. soft butter
3 squares unsweetened chocolate, melted and cooled

Combine all ingredients in mixer. Beat until smooth. *Will frost and fill 2 layers (8 inch).*

CHOCOLATE SUPREME ICING

A brownie topping.

2 C. sifted confectioners' sugar
¼ tsp. salt
1 egg
⅓ C. soft butter
2 sq. (2 oz.) unsweetened chocolate, melted

Put all ingredients into mixing bowl. Beat until fluffy. *Will frost 1 pan of brownies (8 x 8 x 2 inches).*

CHOCOLATE YOLK FROSTING

Dark and creamy.

6 squares unsweetened chocolate (6 oz.)
3 C. sifted confectioners' sugar
5 tbsp. water
6 egg yolks
½ C. soft butter

Melt chocolate over hot water. Remove from heat. Stir in sugar and water. Add egg yolks, beating well. Add butter, and beat until smooth. *Will frost and fill a 3-layer cake.*

CHRISTMAS COOKIE FROSTING

For sugar cookies or butter cookies.

2 egg whites
¼ tsp. cream of tartar
¼ tsp. vanilla
2½ C. sifted confectioners' sugar

Beat egg whites, cream of tartar, and vanilla until foamy. Gradually beat in sugar until frosting stands in firm peaks. Frost cookies. Decorate as desired.

CINNAMON DRIBBLE GLAZE

To top the poppy seed cake.

1 tsp. butter
2 tbsp. hot milk
1½ C. confectioners' sugar
½ tsp. vanilla
½ tsp. cinnamon
¼ tsp. salt

Add butter to milk. Mix in sugar, vanilla, cinnamon, and salt. Beat well. Pour or spread on cake.

CINNAMON-SUGAR MIXTURE

Toast, cinnamon rolls, etc.

1 C. sugar
⅓ C. cinnamon

Mix until blended. Keep in tightly fitted jar.

COCOA WHIPPED CREAM

For filling or covering a cake.

1½ C. heavy cream
⅓ C. cocoa
½ C. sugar

Combine ingredients. Chill 1 hour. Beat until stiff. *Will cover 2 layers (8 inch).*

PLAIN CONFECTIONERS' OR LEMON BUTTER ICING

2 C. sifted confectioners' sugar
¼ C. coffee cream
3 tbsp. soft butter
½ tsp. vanilla or rum extract

Beat all together. *Glazes a 10-inch chiffon or angel food cake.* Variation: Substitute ½ teaspoon lemon extract for vanilla.

FLUFFY FROSTING

Deliciously smooth.

¼ tsp. salt
2 egg whites
½ C. sugar
1 C. corn syrup, light or dark
1 tsp. vanilla

Add salt to egg whites. Beat until soft peaks form. Add 1 tablespoon sugar at a time, beating until smooth and glossy after each addition. Add corn syrup, a little at a time. Beat thoroughly. Add vanilla. Continue beating until frosting stands in stiff, firm peaks. *Will frost 3 layers (9 inch).*

FLUFFY MERINGUE

For pies? For baked Alaskas?

FOR 8- OR 9-INCH PIE
3 egg whites
¼ tsp. cream of tartar
6 tbsp. sugar
½ tsp. vanilla

FOR 10-INCH PIE
4 egg whites
½ tsp. cream of tartar
½ C. sugar
¾ tsp. vanilla

Beat egg whites and cream of tartar until soft peaks
form. Add sugar gradually while beating. Blend in vanilla.
Beat to stiff-and-glossy stage. Variations: (1) Substitute
brown sugar for granulated sugar on butterscotch pies.
(2) Substitute various flavorings or liquors for vanilla.
Examples: lemon pie—lemon extract; lime pie—lime extract; chocolate pie—rum extract. Hint: Bake meringue
at 375°F. for 15 to 20 minutes. Cool away from drafts.
Do not refrigerate. Always spread meringue over hot
fillings and to the edge. Cool pie 3 to 4 hours after meringue has been baked. Cut with knife dipped in hot water.

FRUITCAKE GLAZE

A shiny coat.

¼ C. unsweetened pineapple (or other) juice
½ C. light corn syrup

Bring to boil. Remove from heat. Brush on fruit cake.
Decorate cake with crystalline fruit. Add second coat of
glaze.

GLAZE

To brush on royal icing cakes to make them shiny.

½ C. cold water
3 tbsp. unflavored gelatin

Put water and gelatin in double boiler. Let melt until clear and hot. Brush on frosted cake.

GLAZES FOR BREAD

1. Egg whites or egg yolks: Mix with 1 teaspoon water, milk, or cream. Brush mixture on 10 minutes before bread is done.

2. Whole egg: Mix 1 egg with 1 teaspoon of milk, cream, or water. Brush mixture on 10 minutes before bread is done.

3. Salad oil: Brush on bread before last rising, or before it goes into the oven.

4. Soft butter: Brush on bread before last rising, or before or after it comes from the oven.

5. Egg yolk: Mix with fork 1 egg yolk and 2 tablespoons cold water, milk, or cream. Brush on just before baking or 10 minutes before bread is done. Gives shiny golden brown finish.

6. Egg white: Beat 1 egg white until foamy, or mix with 1 teaspoon water, milk, or cream. Brush on before baking, or 10 minutes before bread is done.

7. Honey topping: Beat ¼ cup butter, ⅔ cup confectioners' sugar, 1 egg white, and 2 tablespoons honey all together until smooth. Brush on bread after it has been shaped.

8. Starch glaze: Dissolve 1 teaspoon cornstarch in ¼ cup water in a saucepan. Add 1 cup water and bring to a boil. Brush on hot baked bread. Can be stored in a jar in refrigerator.

JIFFY FROSTING

For washday blues.

   3 egg whites
   ½ C. jelly or ¼ C. honey

Beat egg whites until they begin to hold shape. Add jelly or honey gradually until frosting stands stiff in peaks. *Will frost a 3-layer cake.*

MAPLE FROSTING

Perfect for spice cakes.

   ¾ C. brown sugar, packed
   2½ tbsp. water
   1 egg white
   ¼ tsp. maple flavoring

Cook sugar, water, and egg white in double boiler. Beat constantly until mixture forms peaks. Remove from heat. Add maple flavoring. Beat until of spreading consistency. *Will frost 2 layers (8 inch).* Double the recipe for 3 layers. Top with ground nuts.

MOCK CARAMEL FILLING OR TOPPING

It's easy! It's different!

   1 can condensed milk (13 oz.)
   ½ C. finely chopped nuts*

Submerge can of milk in boiling water. Simmer 1 hour. Let cool in refrigerator overnight. Open can. Spread on loaf cake (13 x 9 x 2 inches) or fill 2-layer cake (8 inches). Can be mixed with nuts.

* *Optional.*

MOCK WHIPPING CREAM ICING

Would you believe it?

½ C. butter
½ C. vegetable shortening
1 C. sugar
1 egg white
1 tsp. vanilla
¾ C. scalded milk, cooled

Cream butter and shortening. Add sugar gradually while mixing. Beat in egg white and vanilla. Cream thoroughly. Add milk slowly. *Will frost and fill a 3-layer cake.*

NUT FILLING

'Tween spicy layers.

2 egg whites
2 tbsp. confectioners' sugar
1 C. chopped hickory nuts (or any other kind)

Beat egg whites until medium stiff. Add sugar. Continue beating until stiff. Fold in nuts. Use as a filling for spice cake.

PASTRY CREAM

A filling for cream puffs.

1 tbsp. unflavored gelatin
¼ C. cold water
⅔ C. sugar

½ C. flour
4 egg yolks
2 C. milk, scalded
1 tsp. vanilla
4 egg whites
¼ C. sugar

Dissolve gelatin in cold water. Mix together the ⅔ cup sugar and the flour. Beat in yolks. Gradually add scalded milk. Cook until thickened. Remove from heat. Add vanilla and gelatin. Stir until dissolved. Cover and refrigerate until it starts to set. Beat egg whites until almost stiff. Add ¼ cup sugar and continue to beat until stiff. Fold into custard. Refrigerate until ready to use. *Will fill 1 dozen medium cream puffs.*

PECAN-COCONUT FROSTING

To ice German chocolate, especially.

1 C. butter or margarine
2 C. evaporated milk
2 C. sugar
6 egg yolks
2 tsp. vanilla
2⅔ C. flaked coconut
2 C. chopped pecans

Melt butter and heat to boiling point. Add milk, sugar, egg yolks, and vanilla. Cook and stir over medium heat until thickened, about 12 minutes. Add coconut and pecans. Beat until thick enough to spread. *Makes 5 cups.* Can be refrigerated up to 2 weeks.

PIE GLAZES

After baking a 2-crust pie, let it cool, brush with warm corn syrup, and sprinkle with 1 tablespoon granulated sugar. Brown quickly and sprinkle again with 1 tablespoon sugar.

For an apple pie, brush with warm corn syrup, sprinkle with 2 tablespoons raisins, and then with 2 tablespoons cinnamon-sugar mixture. Do not brown.

ROYAL ICING

To be used in cake or cookie decorating.

MADE WITH EGG WHITES
2 egg whites, room temperature
2 C. sifted confectioners' sugar
1 tsp. cream of tartar

MADE WITH MERINGUE POWDER
1/4 C. meringue powder
3 C. sifted confectioners' sugar
1/2 C. hot water
1/2 tsp. cream of tartar

Place all ingredients in a mixing bowl, and beat 8 to 10 minutes on high speed. Cover with a damp cloth while decorating to prevent crust forming. Note: One teaspoon glycerin may be added to the icing to keep it soft on the cake.

SEA FOAM FROSTING

Can be tinted.

    1 C. sugar
    ½ C. brown sugar, packed
    ¼ tsp. cream of tartar
    ¼ C. water
    ⅛ tsp. salt
    2 egg whites

Boil sugars, cream of tartar, and water to 242°F. Remove from heat. Beat egg whites with salt. Add syrup slowly while beating. Continue to beat until mixture is cold and holds its shape. *Will frost a 2-layer cake (9 inch).*

SHINY GLAZE

For trimmings.

    3 C. sifted confectioners' sugar
    4 tsp. light corn syrup
    ¼ C. hot water
    ⅛ tsp. salt
    ½ tsp. lemon or vanilla extract
    Food coloring, if desired

Mix all ingredients until smooth and glossy. Lay cookies on rack over pan. Brush or pour glaze over them. Add a few drops of hot water to thin glaze as necessary. Let dry 1 hour. Decorate or paint with food coloring.

STRAWBERRY-BANANA ICING

Quick, no-cook frosting for gingerbread or spice cake.

½ C. fresh strawberries
½ C. ripe mashed bananas
½ C. sugar
1 egg white
Dash of salt

With electric mixer, combine all ingredients. Beat until thick and fluffy, about 8 minutes. *Makes 5 cups, which will frost 3 layers (8 inch).*

TIP TOP MERINGUE

Make roses, cover pie shells, or just anything.

2¼ C. sugar
1 C. water
1 C. egg whites

Boil sugar and water to 240°F. Beat the egg whites until they are very stiff. Add syrup slowly, beating constantly. Continue beating until cool. Put through decorating tube or spread on pies.

Pies

Whenever I make a huckleberry pie, I think of the big patches of berries that grew on our hillside. When the berries were in season, Mother would get up early, hurry with the housework, and then go to the huckleberry patch. She would stay until she picked ten quarts. "Two for supper, and eight to can," she would say.

When I was too small to pick without stepping on the tender vines, I would make myself useful carrying fresh spring water to Mother, and spreading the lunch so we could eat together. Afterwards I would wander in the woods, but always within call.

Mother was so proud of all her fruits, and her quota of huckleberries was never less than one-hundred quarts. This gave us plenty for pies and sauces through the winter months of this one favorite. She also canned cherries and strawberries, which were plentiful, and apples from our orchard.

Often after a canning day Mother would light a candle and go down to survey the cellar. Sweeping the dim light across the neatly labeled jars gave her the satisfaction of knowing there was plenty of everything to "winter us through." She canned most of our meat and vege-

tables, too, and often lost count when taking a total of
her stock; for each time she added to it, she would start
counting all over again.

Today we can shop in our supermarkets and buy fruit
already prepared for pies. Looking at these wide assort-
ments, I often remember the old days: berries filling the
tin pail, juice-stained fingers, and the fragrance of bub-
bling fruit. But most of all, I remember Mother.

AUTUMN PEACH PIE

The last from the orchard, when the leaves are falling.

FILLING
    5 C. sliced fresh peaches
    ⅔ C. sugar
    ¾ tsp. nutmeg
    ½ tsp. cinnamon
    ½ tsp. almond extract
    2 tbsp. lemon juice
    1 tbsp. butter
    3 tbsp. tapioca
    Pastry for 8-inch 2-crust pie

TOPPING
    2 tbsp. heavy cream
    3 tbsp. sugar

Mix all filling ingredients. Turn into pastry-lined pie
pan. Cover with top crust which has slits in it. Seal and
flute. Brush cream on top of pie crust. Sprinkle with the
3 tablespoons sugar. Bake in preheated oven (425°F.)
for 50 to 60 minutes, or until bubbly. *Serves 6.*

CHOCOLATE BAVARIAN PIE

Tyrolean masterpiece.

1½ tsp. unflavored gelatin
¼ C. cold water
½ C. boiling water
1 C. chocolate milk
1½ C. heavy cream
1 C. confectioners' sugar
¼ C. Dutch cocoa
1 baked pastry shell (8 inch)

Soften gelatin in cold water. Add the boiling water. Stir in chocolate milk. Set over crushed ice and stir until it is like unbeaten egg whites. Beat cream. Fold in the confectioners' sugar and cocoa. Add to the gelatin mixture. Keep over ice until mixture has the consistency of soft mounds. Pile into pastry shell. Chill, and decorate.

CHOCOLATE FUDGE BANANA PIE

It's a snap.

1 package (5½ oz.) chocolate fudge pudding
3 C. hot chocolate milk
2 medium bananas
1 baked pie shell (9 inch)
Whipped cream for garnish

Combine pudding mix and chocolate milk. Cook over medium heat, stirring constantly, until mixture comes to a full boil. Cool slightly. Slice bananas into pie shell. Pour pudding mixture on top. Refrigerate 3 hours. Garnish with whipped cream. *Serves 6 to 8.*

CITY APPLE PIE

Serve with cheddar cheese or vanilla ice cream.

    5 C. canned, sliced apples
    ⅔ C. sugar
    ⅓ C. light brown sugar, packed
    1 tsp. cinnamon
    ¼ tsp. nutmeg
    Pastry for 9-inch 2-crust pie
    ¼ tsp. salt
    1 tbsp. lemon juice
    2 tbsp. butter
    3 tbsp. minute tapioca
    ¼ tsp. allspice

Mix all ingredients except crust together. Turn into pastry-lined pie pan. Cover with top crust which has slits cut in top. Seal and flute. Bake in preheated oven (425°F.) for 20 minutes; then reduce temperature to 375°F. and continue to bake for 30 to 40 minutes longer. *Serves 8.*

FRESH STRAWBERRY SPONGE PIE

A summer berry special.

    2 C. slightly crushed fresh strawberries
    ¼ C. sugar
    1 tbsp. unflavored gelatin
    ¾ C. cold water
    1 tbsp. lemon juice
    ⅛ tsp. salt
    ½ C. heavy cream, whipped
    2 egg whites, beaten stiff
    ¼ tsp. red food coloring
    1 baked pastry shell (8 inch), cooled

Sprinkle sugar on berries. Let stand 30 minutes. Dissolve gelatin in cold water. Melt over hot water. Cool. Add strawberry mixture, lemon juice, and salt. Chill until partially set. Fold in whipped cream, egg whites, and coloring. Chill 15 minutes, in refrigerator. Pour into pastry shell. Chill 3 hours. Garnish with whipped cream and fresh berries. *Serves 6.*

FROZEN PUMPKIN PIE

My first freezer boasted of these no-bake, delicious pies.

    1 C. canned pumpkin
    ½ C. sugar
    ½ tsp. salt
    ½ tsp. nutmeg
    ½ tsp. ginger
    1 qt. French vanilla ice cream
    1 baked pastry shell (9 inch)
    Pecan or walnut halves
    Whipped cream

Mix pumpkin, sugar, salt, nutmeg, ginger, and ice cream until ice cream is softened. Pile into pastry shell and freeze 4 hours. Decorate with whipped cream and pecan halves. *Serves 8.*

GRAPE CHIFFON PIE

Blackberry or raspberry.

    2 tbsp. lemon juice
    1¼ C. grape, blackberry, or raspberry juice
    1 tbsp. unflavored gelatin
    ⅓ C. sugar
    1 pt. rich vanilla ice cream
    1 baked pastry shell (9 inch), cooled

Bring lemon and grape juice to boiling point. Remove from heat. Add gelatin and sugar. Stir until gelatin dissolves. Stir in ice cream until it melts. Pour into pastry shell. Chill 3 hours. Garnish with whipped cream and toasted sliced almonds.

GREEN GOOSEBERRY PIE

The berries will come from Canada.

5 C. gooseberries
1 C. sugar
4 tsp. tapioca
1 tsp. cinnamon
⅛ tsp. salt
1 tbsp. butter, melted
1 unbaked pastry shell (9 in.)
Lattice top

Mix berries, sugar, tapioca, cinnamon, salt, and butter. Fill pastry shell. Cover with lattice strips. Bake in preheated oven (425°F.) for 30 minutes; reduce heat to 375°F. and continue baking for 15 to 20 minutes. When pie comes from the oven, sprinkle about 2 tablespoons sugar on top.

IRISH WHISKEY PIE

The dessert that outsells all the others at the Farmer's
Daughter Restaurant in Orland Park, Illinois.

1½ tsp. unflavored gelatin
½ C. cold water
2 sq. unsweetened chocolate
½ C. hot water
¼ tsp. salt
½ C. sugar
¼ C. egg yolks
¼ C. milk
3 tbsp. Irish whiskey
¼ C. egg whites
1 C. heavy cream, whipped
¼ C. sliced almonds
1 baked pastry shell (9 inch), chilled

Dissolve gelatin in cold water. Combine chocolate, hot
water, salt, and sugar. Bring to boil and cook until smooth.
Mix egg yolks and milk. Stir into chocolate mixture. Melt
gelatin over hot water until clear. Add to chocolate mixture with whiskey. Pour into mixing bowl and place over
crushed ice until syrupy. Beat egg whites and fold in. Fold
in whipped cream and almonds. Chill 4 hours. Garnish
with additional whipped cream and sliced almonds. *Serves
6 to 8.*

LEMON NECTAR PIE

Ambrosial chiffon.

4 tsp. unflavored gelatin
⅓ C. cold water
5 egg yolks
⅓ C. lemon juice

1 tsp. lemon extract
¾ C. sugar
1 tsp. salt
2 C. heavy cream, whipped
¼ tsp. yellow food coloring
1 baked pastry shell (8 inch)

Soften gelatin in cold water. Melt over hot water. Beat egg yolks. Add lemon juice, extract, sugar, salt, and melted gelatin. Chill until consistency of unbeaten egg whites. Fold in whipped cream and food coloring. Pile into pastry shell. Variations: (1) Crème de Menthe Parfait Pie: Add 2 teaspoons crème de menthe to lemon juice, and substitute green for yellow food coloring. (2) Orange Nectar Pie: Substitute orange juice for lemon juice, extract, and food coloring.

LEMONADE PIE

Or it could be limeade.

1 tbsp. unflavored gelatin
½ C. cold water
4 egg yolks, beaten
⅛ tsp. salt
1 can (6 oz.) frozen lemonade concentrate
4 egg whites
½ C. sugar
½ C. heavy cream, whipped
¼ tsp. yellow food coloring
1 baked pastry shell (9 inch), cooled

Dissolve gelatin in cold water. Melt in double boiler. Add eggs and salt. Cook and stir until mixture is slightly thickened. Add concentrate and chill. Beat egg whites until soft peaks form. Gradually add sugar, beating to stiff peaks. Fold in gelatin mixture and whipped cream with a wire whip. Add yellow food coloring for a lemonade pie, or green for limeade. Pile into pastry shell. Chill until firm.

OLD SETTLER LEMON RAISIN PIE

"Never heard of it?"

    2 C. raisins
    4 C. cold water
    ½ lemon, sliced thin and halved
    ¼ tsp. salt
    ½ C. sugar
    2 tbsp. tapioca
    1 unbaked pastry shell (8 inch)
    Lattice top

Soak raisins overnight in the water with lemon. Drain, but reserve 2 cups of juice. Heat to boiling point, and while stirring add salt, sugar, and tapioca. Simmer 5 minutes. Add raisins and lemon. Chill until cool, 1 to 2 hours. Pour into chilled unbaked pastry shell. Top with lattice strips. Bake in preheated oven (425°F.) for 35 minutes or until golden brown.

ORANGE BAVARIAN PIE

Taste of the Alps.

    1 tbsp. unflavored gelatin
    ¾ C. cold water
    1 C. orange juice
    1½ tsp. pure orange extract
    1 tbsp. lemon juice
    ¼ tsp. orange coloring
    1 C. heavy cream, whipped
    ½ C. confectioners' sugar
    1 baked pastry shell (8 inch)

Soften gelatin in ¼ cup water. Dissolve over boiling water. Add ½ cup water, orange juice, orange extract, lemon juice, and orange coloring to gelatin. Place pan over cold water with ice cubes. Let set until it is the consistency of unbeaten egg whites. Stir in confectioners' sugar to the whipped cream. Fold cream mixture into gelatin mixture. Fill baked pastry shell. Chill 3 hours. Decorate as desired. *Serves 6.*

PAPER-SHELL PECAN PIE

The favorite of the president from Missouri and delivered to him in Independence for many years.

½ C. soft butter
1 C. sugar
3 eggs, slightly beaten
¾ C. dark corn syrup
¼ tsp. salt
1 tsp. vanilla
1 C. coarsely chopped pecans
1 unbaked pastry shell (8 inch)

Chill pastry shell 1 hour. Cream butter and sugar. Stir in eggs, corn syrup, salt, vanilla, and pecans. Pour into pastry shell. Bake on lower rack in preheated oven (375°F.) for 45 to 50 minutes. Serve with French vanilla ice cream. *Serves 6.*

PILGRIM PUMPKIN PIE

Great Grandma's recipe.

1½ C. pumpkin
¾ C. sugar
1 tsp. cinnamon
¼ tsp. cloves
2 tbsp. vegetable oil

Pies   281

1½ C. coffee cream
2 eggs, beaten
½ tsp. ginger
¾ tsp. salt
1 unbaked pastry shell (9 inch)

Mix all ingredients. Pour into pastry shell. Bake in preheated oven (425°F.) for 45 to 55 minutes. To test, insert knife in center; if it comes out clean, pie is done. Cool and top with whipped cream when ready to serve. *Serves 8.*

RED RASPBERRY CHIFFON PIE

Fresh or frozen berries.

¼ C. lemon juice, fresh, canned, or frozen
¼ C. water
½ C. sugar
4 egg yolks, well beaten
1 tbsp. unflavored gelatin
¼ C. cold water
1 C. crushed fresh red raspberries
1 C. whole fresh red raspberries
4 egg whites
½ C. sugar
¼ tsp. red food coloring
1 baked pastry shell (10 inch)

Cook in double boiler the lemon juice, ¼ cup water, ½ cup sugar, and egg yolks. Stir in gelatin that has been softened in the remaining ¼ cup cold water. Add crushed berries. Chill until partially set. Beat egg whites until stiff, adding the remaining ½ cup sugar. Fold in the whole berries, food coloring, and the egg yolk mixture. Pile into pastry shell. Chill and decorate. Substitution for

fresh berries: 1 12-oz. package of frozen berries (drained).
Do not add berries to gelatin mixture, but fold all of them
into stiffly beaten egg whites. Leave out sugar in egg
whites if berries have been in syrup.

SOUR CREAM CHEESE PIE

Make two—to have and to hold.

    3 C. graham cracker crumbs
    ½ C. butter, melted
    ⅓ C. sugar
    5 C. cream cheese (5 8-oz. packages)
    1 C. sugar
    1 tsp. vanilla
    3 eggs
    2 C. sour cream
    ½ C. sugar

Mix cracker crumbs, butter, and ⅓ cup sugar in mixer.
Press into 2 pie pans (10 inch). Chill 1 hour. Beat cream
cheese, 1 cup sugar, and vanilla until creamy. Add eggs
one at a time, and continue beating. Divide in the 2 pie
pans. Bake in preheated oven (375°F.) for 25 minutes.
Cool 20 minutes. Mix sour cream and ½ cup sugar.
Divide and spread on top of the 2 pies. Bake in preheated oven (475°F.) for 10 minutes. Cool. Refrigerate
3 hours. Serve plain or with canned cherry pie mix.
Freeze one.

STRAWBERRY-BANANA GELATIN PIE

More than slightly different.

1 baked pastry shell (8 inch)
1 package (3 oz.) strawberry gelatin
1 C. boiling water
¾ C. cold water
1 C. sliced bananas
½ C. sliced fresh strawberries

Dissolve gelatin in boiling water. Add cold water. Chill until syrupy. Fold in fruit. Pour into pastry shell. Chill until firm. Top with whipped cream. *Serves 6.*

STRAWBERRY-RHUBARB PIE

Cut stalks when they are red.

1⅓ C. sugar
¼ tsp. salt
¼ tsp. nutmeg
2 tbsp. tapioca
¼ C. orange juice
2 tbsp. butter
4 C. ½-inch rhubarb pieces
1 C. strawberry halves
1 unbaked pastry shell (8 inch) with plain or lattice top

Combine filling ingredients. Fill pastry shell. Cover with plain or lattice top. Brush with milk and sprinkle 2 tablespoons sugar on top. Bake in preheated oven (450°F.) for 25 minutes; reduce heat to 375°F. for 20 to 25 minutes.

TOASTED COCONUT ORANGE PIE

A dessert as inviting as . . . an Hawaiian sunset.

1 baked pastry shell (8 inch)
1 package (3¼ oz.) coconut cream pudding
1 C. orange juice
2 tbsp. sugar
¾ C. water
1 tsp. orange extract

Bring orange juice, water, and sugar to boil. Add pudding mix and boil 1 minute. Stir in orange extract. Cool 10 minutes. Pour into pastry shell. Refrigerate 3 hours. Decorate with whipped cream and toasted coconut.

WINTER MINCEMEAT PIE

Serve me warm.

3½ C. canned mincemeat
1 C. diced apples
½ tsp. cinnamon
½ tsp. allspice
¼ C. lemon juice
1 tsp. orange flavor
¼ C. brandy or rum
¼ C. maraschino cherry halves
2 tsp. tapioca
1 tbsp. butter
Pastry for 2-crust pie (8 inch)

Mix filling ingredients and turn into pastry-lined pie pan. Cover with top crust; cut slits in top. Bake in pre-heated oven (425°F.) 40 to 45 minutes.

PERFECT PIE CRUST

Keep it in a ball in the refrigerator.

3 C. sifted cake flour
1 tsp. salt
1 C. lard (render your own)
5 tbsp. warm water
2¼ tsp. sugar

Combine flour and salt. Cut in lard with pastry blender until it is like fine meal. Dissolve sugar in warm water and cool in refrigerator for 20 minutes. Add water to flour mixture and mix with a fork until well blended. Turn out onto a lightly floured board and roll to desired thickness. *Will make one 8-inch two-crust pie and 1 bottom crust.* Bake two-crust pie according to recipe. For the one-crust pie, set another pie tin (one that has been greased on the bottom) inside the crust to hold it in shape. Bake in pre-heated oven (450°F.) for 10 minutes. Remove the pie tin and finish baking at 400°F. until brown.

CHOCOLATE-COCONUT CRUST

A candylike shell.

2 sq. (2 oz.) unsweetened chocolate
2 tbsp. butter
2 tbsp. coffee cream, warmed
⅔ C. sifted confectioners' sugar
1½ C. shredded coconut

Melt chocolate and butter over low heat. Add cream and sugar. Stir well. Fold in coconut. Press into a lightly greased pie pan (8 inch). Chill until firm. May be filled with peppermint ice cream. Decorate with whipped cream.

GRAHAM CRACKER CRUST

For an 8- or 9-inch pie.

    1½ C. graham cracker crumbs
    2½ tbsp. sugar
    2 tbsp. all-purpose flour
    ⅓ C. butter, melted

Mix all ingredients thoroughly. Press mixture firmly and evenly against sides and bottom of pie pan. Bake in preheated oven (350°F.) for 8 to 10 minutes. Cool and fill with Spanish Brandy Cheese Cake,* or as desired.

MERINGUE SHELL

Hot weather ice cream pie.

    2 egg whites
    ⅛ tsp. salt
    ⅛ tsp. cream of tartar
    ½ C. sugar
    ½ tsp. vanilla
    ½ C. chopped walnuts or pecans (optional)
    ½ tsp. food coloring
    1½ to 2 qt. peppermint ice cream
    Heavy cream, whipped for garnish
    Peppermint candy shavings

Beat egg whites with salt and cream of tartar until foamy. Add sugar gradually. Continue to beat to stiff peaks. Fold in vanilla, nuts, and coloring. Spread into lightly greased and floured pie pan (8 inch), building sides up ½ inch above edge of pan. Bake in slow preheated oven (200°F.) for 50 to 55 minutes until light

* See *Index.*

golden in color. Fill with peppermint ice cream. Freeze until serving time. *Makes 8 servings.* When ready to serve, decorate with whipped cream and peppermint candy shavings.

MERINGUE SHELLS

Color them pink for pretty.

Use 1 recipe Angel Meringue*
½ tsp. red food coloring

Beat food coloring into Angel Meringue. Drop meringue by ⅓ cupfuls onto baking sheet lined with brown paper. Shape mounds into circles, building up sides. Bake in preheated oven (275°F.) for 1 hour. Turn off heat and leave shells in closed oven for approximately 1½ hours. Cool away from drafts. *Makes 8 to 10 colorful shells.* Fill with scoops of ice cream before serving. Top with fresh strawberries. Variation: Add ½ cup finely chopped walnuts or pecans.

* See *Index.*

Desserts

APPLE BROWN BETTY

For a sixsome.

    2 C. canned apples
    1 C. soft white bread cubes
    ¾ C. light brown sugar, packed
    ¼ tsp. salt
    ½ tsp. nutmeg
    ½ tsp. cinnamon
    ⅓ C. butter, melted
    ½ C. water
    1 tbsp. lemon juice

Place one layer of sliced apples in buttered 1-quart casserole. Spread ½ of bread cubes over apples. Combine sugar, salt, nutmeg, and cinnamon. Sprinkle ½ of the sugar mixture over bread cubes. Pour ½ of the butter over the sugar layer. Repeat layers with the other half of the ingredients. Combine water and lemon juice and pour over mixture. Bake in preheated oven (350°F.) for 45 to 50 minutes. Serve warm with packaged lemon sauce, cream, or whipped cream. *Serves 6.*

BREAD PUDDING

The oldest of American desserts.

4 C. 1- or 2-day-old bread
2 tbsp. butter, melted
½ C. sugar
½ C. scalded seedless raisins
3 C. warmed milk
3 whole eggs
1 tsp. vanilla
Pinch cinnamon
Pinch nutmeg

Cut bread in 1-inch cubes (leave crust on). Place in a bowl. Add eggs to milk. Blend. Add sugar, raisins, butter, cinnamon, and nutmeg and blend together. Pour over bread. Allow to soak 4 to 5 minutes. Place in buttered 1½-quart baking dish. Sprinkle with nutmeg. Set baking dish in a pan of hot water. Bake in preheated oven (350°F.) for 1 hour or until custard is set. Serve warm with warmed coffee cream.

CORNSTARCH PUDDING

Pie or cake filling.

¼ C. butter
½ C. cornstarch
1½ C. sugar
½ tsp. salt
4 C. hot milk
4 egg yolks, beaten slightly
¼ tsp. yellow food coloring
1 tbsp. vanilla

Melt butter. Blend in cornstarch, sugar, and salt. Stir in milk gradually. Heat to simmer. Remove from heat. Mix in egg yolk and food coloring. Cook until thickened. Remove from heat and add vanilla. Pour into 8 custard cups or 9-inch baked pastry shell; or cool and use as cake filling.

CREAM PUFF DOUGH

Zephyr light.

    ½ C. butter
    1 C. water
    ¼ tsp. salt
    1 tsp. sugar
    1 C. flour
    4 eggs

Put butter, water, salt, and sugar into saucepan. Heat until butter melts. Reduce heat. Stir in flour until ball forms. Remove from heat and put into mixer bowl. Beat in eggs one at a time. Put dough into pastry tube with a ½-inch nozzle. Squeeze out ½ inch for miniature cream puffs (or 3 inches for eclairs, or 2 inch balls for cream puffs) onto ungreased cookie sheets. Bake in preheated oven (450°F.) for 15 minutes; then reduce heat to 350°F. and bake miniatures for 5 minutes, eclairs for 20 minutes, and cream puffs for 25 minutes. Cool away from drafts. Cut off tops and pull out soft dough. Fill and replace tops. Dust with confectioners' sugar. Refrigerate. *Makes 12 large cream puffs*. Filling: May be vanilla pudding, whipped cream, custard, or hors d'oeuvre dip.

CUP CUSTARD

Serve warm or chilled.

2½ C. milk
¼ C. sugar
⅛ tsp. salt
3 eggs, slightly beaten
1 tsp. vanilla
⅛ tsp. nutmeg

Scald milk, sugar, and salt. Pour over eggs, vanilla, and nutmeg, stirring constantly. Pour into 6 individual molds. Place molds in a pan containing about 1 inch of hot water. Sprinkle top with additional nutmeg. Bake in preheated oven (350°F.) for 1 hour or until the custard is set. Variation: For Caramelized Custard, melt in heavy skillet ½ cup sugar. Stir slowly and constantly until golden. Spoon a little into each mold, tilting to glaze cup. Pour in custard. Proceed as above for baking. Chill 3 hours. Turn upside down on individual serving plates. Serve plain or with whipped cream.

FLAMBED BANANAS

A creative dessert that makes a dinner party memorable.

¼ C. butter
2 tbsp. light brown sugar, packed
¼ C. light corn syrup
2 tsp. lemon extract
4 bananas, cut into halves
¼ C. Cointreau
4 large scoops French vanilla ice cream

Melt butter in skillet. Stir in sugar, corn syrup, and lemon extract. Heat until bubbly. Add bananas. Coat with glaze. Pour in Cointreau. Ignite and stir. Serve over ice cream. *Serves 4.*

FRESH PEACH JUBILEE

Midnight dessert.

> ½ C. butter
> 2 tbsp. light brown sugar
> ¼ C. light corn syrup
> 6 to 8 peaches, peeled, seeded, and quartered
> ¼ C. rum
> ¼ C. peach liquor

Melt butter and sugar in chafing dish. Add syrup, and cook until bubbly. Add peaches, and baste for 1 minute. Pour in rum and peach liquor. Ignite. Stir, moving peaches to sides of chafing dish (flame will be higher and more effective). Serve over 6 French vanilla ice cream balls. *Serves 4 to 6.* Hint: Have a high flame under chafing dish, or rum and liquor will not ignite.

LIME CHIFFON GELATIN

Make it any party flavor.

> 1 C. cold water
> 2 tsp. unflavored gelatin
> 2 packages (3 oz.) lime gelatin
> 2 tbsp. sugar
> ¼ tsp. salt
> 2 C. boiling water
> 2 C. coffee cream
> 1 tsp. vanilla
> 1 C. commercial sour cream

Dissolve unflavored gelatin in cold water. Dissolve lime gelatin, sugar, and salt in boiling water. Add unflavored gelatin mixture, cream, vanilla, and sour cream. Stir until smooth. Refrigerate until slightly thickened. Whip until smooth. Pour into lightly greased 2-quart mold. Chill 4 hours. Unmold. Decorate with whipped cream. *Serves 10 to 12.*

OLD-FASHIONED RICE PUDDING

Great-Grandmother gathered rice seeds for this one.

¼ C. raisins
½ C. water
4 eggs, slightly beaten
½ C. sugar
1 tsp. vanilla
2¾ C. cooked rice
¾ tsp. salt
2 C. milk, scalded
Nutmeg

Simmer raisins in ½ cup water for 5 minutes. Drain. Combine eggs, sugar, vanilla, rice, and salt. Add milk slowly while stirring. Pour into a well-greased 1½-quart casserole. Sprinkle with nutmeg. Place in a pan of hot water. Bake in a preheated oven (325°F.) for 1½ hours or until the blade of a knife comes out clean when tested in center. Serve warm with heavy or coffee cream. *Serves 10.* May be reheated before serving.

PEACH COBBLER

Little feet will run for this.

2 C. sliced peaches
2 tbsp. flour
¼ C. sugar
2 tbsp. lemon juice
¾ C. fruit syrup
1 tbsp. butter
1½ C. sifted all-purpose flour
½ tsp. baking powder
1 tbsp. sugar
⅓ C. margarine
1 egg, beaten
½ C. milk

Arrange fruit in greased round cake pan (8 inch). Mix 2 tablespoons flour with ¼ cup sugar. Sprinkle over fruit. Add lemon juice and fruit syrup. Dot with butter. Heat in oven at 425°F. for 10 minutes. Sift remaining dry ingredients together. Cut in margarine. Mix egg and milk. Add to dry ingredients. Stir. Drop dough in 6 to 8 mounds over fruit. Bake in preheated oven (425°F.) for 30 minutes. Top with whipped cream before serving. Best when warm or reheated in 350°F. oven for 15 minutes. *Serves 8.*

PERSIMMON PUDDING

A favorite in the Midwest, where the small wild persimmons grow in profusion but must be touched with frost before they are picked.

2 eggs
¾ C. sugar
1 pt. persimmon pulp, peeled and diced
1 pt. milk

¼ C. butter, melted
½ tsp. baking soda
2 C. sifted all-purpose flour
1 tsp. baking powder
¼ tsp. cinnamon
¼ tsp. nutmeg
¼ tsp. salt
¾ C. chopped black walnuts or pecans

Beat egg and sugar. Add persimmon pulp, milk, and butter. Sift dry ingredients and add to egg mixture. Stir in nuts. Pour into a greased square pan (8 x 8 x 2 inches). Bake in preheated oven (350°F.) for 40 minutes. Top with whipped cream or Pour Custard.* *Serves 8 to 10.*

PRUNE DUFF

Great Grandmother used to boil this pudding in a cloth bag.

PUDDING
2 eggs
½ C. margarine, melted
1 C. brown sugar, packed
1½ C. pitted cooked prunes
1 C. sifted all-purpose flour
½ tsp. salt
1 tsp. soda
1 tbsp. cool milk

* See *Index.*

SAUCE

3 tbsp. cornstarch
⅔ C. sugar
2 C. prune juice
2 tbsp. lemon juice
1 tbsp. butter
⅛ tsp. nutmeg

Beat eggs. Add brown sugar and margarine. Stir in prunes, flour, and salt. Melt soda in milk. Add to batter. Fill 1½-qt. greased pudding mold. Cover and steam one hour. Serve hot with pudding sauce. May be made a day or two before and steamed again for 10 minutes. To make sauce, mix cornstarch, sugar, and juices. Cook over low heat until thickened, stirring frequently. Remove from heat and blend in butter and nutmeg. Pour over pudding, and it's ready to serve.

PRUNE WHIP

Mom's way.

1 C. prune juice
1 tbsp. cornstarch
⅓ C. sugar
¼ tsp. salt
3 egg whites, beaten
¼ C. chopped walnuts
1 C. cooked, crushed prunes
Thin vanilla pudding (packaged)

Cook prune juice, cornstarch, sugar, and salt until thickened. Cool 20 minutes. Fold in beaten egg whites, nuts, and prunes. Put into 6 to 8 champagne glasses. Refrigerate. Serve with warm thin vanilla pudding. *Serves 6 to 8.*

SPICED APPLESAUCE

A go-together with pork chops.

1½ qt. apple sauce
⅓ C. sugar
¼ C. lemon juice
⅛ tsp. salt
½ tsp. cinnamon
⅛ tsp. allspice

Heat applesauce until boiling. Add sugar, lemon juice, salt, cinnamon, and allspice. Stir until sugar is dissolved. *Serves 10.*

STAINED-GLASS-WINDOW MOLD

'Tis party time in color.

1 package (3 oz.) lime gelatin
1 package (3 oz.) lemon gelatin
1 package (3 oz.) black cherry gelatin
1 package (3 oz.) orange gelatin
6 C. boiling water
⅓ C. unflavored gelatin
½ C. cold water
2 C. pineapple juice
⅓ C. sugar
2 C. heavy cream, whipped to medium stage

Dissolve each gelatin package in 1½ cups boiling water. Pour each into a slightly oiled pan (8 x 8 x 2 inches). Let stand until firm (4 hours). May be refrigerated. Cut into 1-inch cubes. Dissolve unflavored gelatin in cold water. Bring pineapple juice and sugar to boil. Add gelatin (unflavored) and stir until melted. Put in refrigerator or over crushed ice until the consistency of unbeaten egg whites, stirring frequently. Fold in whipped cream and multicolored cubes. Push into 2 slightly oiled molds or loaf pans (9 x 5 x 3 inch). Let set in refrigerator 4 to 6 hours or overnight.

STEAMED PLUM PUDDING

A Christmas tradition.

2 loaves day-old bread
2 tbsp. salt
2 tsp. nutmeg
1 tbsp. cinnamon
1 tsp. cloves
4 C. milk, scalded
2 C. brown sugar, firmly packed
16 eggs, well beaten
2 C. currants
6 C. raisins
2 C. cut dates
1 C. finely sliced citron
1 C. finely sliced candied orange rind
1 lb. ground suet
1 C. orange juice

Remove crusts, and crumb bread. Add salt, spices, milk, and sugar. Mix well. Cool. Stir in eggs, fruits, suet, and orange juice. Mix well. Pour into 2 2-quart heavily greased molds. Cover with lids or foil. Set in pans that contain 2 inches of water. Simmer slowly and steam 5 hours. Watch level of water. Pudding improves with age. Serve with hard sauce, rich pudding sauce, or eggnog sauce. *Each loaf serves 10 to 12.*

UP-TO-DATE RICE SOUFFLÉ

Penny-pincher pudding.

  1 tbsp. unflavored gelatin
  2 tbsp. cold water
  1 C. milk
  1 egg white
  ½ C. sugar
  1 tsp. salt
  2¾ C. cooked rice
  1 tsp. vanilla
  1 C. heavy cream, whipped
  ½ C. candied chopped fruit or chopped nuts*
  Nutmeg*

Dissolve gelatin in cold water in saucepan. Add milk, egg white, sugar, and salt. Cook over medium heat until mixture coats spoon. Remove from heat and cool. Add rice and vanilla. Chill until consistency of unbeaten egg white. Fold in whipped cream. Spoon into glass sherbet dishes. Chill. Variation: Candied chopped fruits or chopped nuts may be added while folding in the whipped cream; or sprinkle top with nutmeg. *Makes 8 to 10 dishes.*

* Optional.

Dessert Sauces

CRÊPE SUZETTE SAUCE

Prepare it at your table.

6 tbsp. sugar
⅔ C. butter
3 tbsp. orange juice
2 tbsp. lemon juice
¼ C. orange Cointreau
¼ C. cognac
2 tbsp. kirsch
1 tbsp. sugar
6 scoops French vanilla ice cream, or 1 C. fresh
    strawberries

Melt 6 tablespoons sugar and butter in skillet (10 inch) over chafing dish. Add juices and heat to simmering. Lay crêpes in juices (also strawberries, if you use them). Heat Cointreau, cognac, and kirsch. Pour over crêpes and ignite. Place 2 crêpes on each heated plate (8 inch). Pour sauce left in skillet over crêpes. Sprinkle the remaining table-spoon of sugar over the 12 crêpes. Add a scoop of ice cream or strawberries to each plate.

PRUNE SAUCE

Over vanilla or lemon pudding.

   3 tbsp. cornstarch
   ⅔ C. sugar
   2 C. prepared prune juice
   2 tbsp. lemon juice
   1 tbsp. butter
   ⅛ tsp. nutmeg

Mix cornstarch and sugar with cold prune and lemon juices. Cook over low heat until thick, stirring frequently to keep from lumping. Remove from heat. Blend in butter and nutmeg. May be made the day before. *Makes approximately 2 cups.*

FRUIT SAUCE AND VARIATIONS

To use on entrées or desserts.

   1½ tbsp. cornstarch
   ⅓ C. sugar
   1 C. fruit juice
   1 tbsp. lemon juice (or variations below)
   1 tsp. butter
   ⅛ tsp. nutmeg

Mix cornstarch and sugar with fruit and lemon juices. Cook over low heat until thick, stirring constantly. Remove from heat. Blend in butter and nutmeg. *Makes 1 cup sauce.* Variations: If using (1) prune juice, serve sauce over vanilla pudding or vanilla cream pie; (2) orange juice, serve over baked ham; (3) apricot or lemon juice, serve over gingerbread squares; (4) strawberry juice, serve over baked Alaska pie; (5) raspberry juice, serve over French vanilla ice cream.

CELIA TUTTLE'S RICH CHRISTMAS HARD SAUCE

Plum pudding, everyone?

  1 C. sifted confectioners' sugar
  2 egg yolks, well beaten
  ¼ C. melted butter
  1 tsp. vanilla extract or 2 tbsp. sherry or brandy (which
      I prefer)
  1 C. heavy cream, whipped

Stir sugar gradually into well-beaten egg yolks. Beat in butter and flavoring. Fold in whipped cream. Serve over Steamed Plum Pudding.* *Makes about 2 cups.*

BOILED POUR CUSTARD

For fresh fruits or puddings.

  1 C. milk
  ½ C. heavy cream
  3 egg yolks
  ¼ C. sugar
  ⅛ tsp. salt
  ¾ tsp. vanilla

* See *Index.*

Heat milk and cream. Beat egg yolks with sugar and salt. Add liquid slowly to eggs. Cook over low heat, stirring constantly with fluffy beat until mixture coats spoon. Remove from heat and stir in vanilla. Cover pan and place in cold water, stirring frequently until cool. Refrigerate until ready to use. *Makes about 1½ cups.*

Miscellaneous

BREADING MIX

For chicken, chops, fish, and what have you.

2 C. sifted all-purpose flour
1 C. commercial Italian bread crumbs
2 tbsp. dry milk
2 tbsp. seasoning salt
5 tsp. paprika

Mix all together.

PREPARING CONVERTED RICE

A staple grain with flavor.

2 tbsp. margarine
1 C. rice
2 C. chicken stock

Sauté rice in margarine until grains are coated. Add stock and cover. Cook over low heat until all liquid is absorbed. *Makes 3 cups.*

SIMPLE SYRUP

2½ C. sugar
1¼ C. water

Combine ingredients in saucepan. Stir over low heat until sugar is dissolved. Cover pan and simmer 2 minutes. Cool. Store in jar. Refrigerate.

SOAP

Homestead style—grease, lye, borax, sugar, salt, ammonia.

A *Farmer's Daughter Cookbook* would not be complete if she forgot to tell you how to make soap. I am sure that modern girls will not take on such a task but might be interested to know how Great Grandmother tackled the job. Each pioneer woman had her own method, and Great Grandma, I am told, made her soap in an iron kettle outdoors. This is hearsay, of course, but others have told me of this primitive way of soap making within their own families. But wouldn't it be fun to try a small batch, if only to please Gram? And the time might come that you would want to make this a hobby, just to surprise your friends with homemade bars of soap. I guarantee this soap will do as fine a job as any commercial brand, but for laundry use only. So today start saving grease that can't be used for cooking.

Now let's pretend that for several months you have watched your grease pail grow. It has reached the top, so now for the big day of soap making. Melt 5 pounds of fat, and strain it thoroughly through a cheesecloth so it will be clear. Don't force it through; let come what may. Take 1 can of lye and dissolve this in 1 quart of cold water, and let it stand until cool. Be careful how you handle this, for we are well aware of its danger. Add the fat slowly to lye water, stirring carefully. Mix 3 teaspoons of borax, 1 teaspoon of salt, 2 tablespoons of sugar, ½ cup of cold water, and ¼ cup of ammonia; add this to the first mixture. Stir all until thick and light colored. If you have any leftover perfume, mix this in too. It is a wonderful way to get rid of those odds and ends of the bottle. Pour into a pan lined with cloth. Indent the desired size before soap becomes hard. When hard, break pieces apart and pile them in such a way that the soap can dry out well.

GUIDE TO MEASURING EQUIVALENTS

3 tsp. = 1 tbsp. = ½ fl. oz.
2 tbsp. = ⅛ C. = 1 fl. oz.
4 tbsp. = ¼ C. = 2 fl. oz.
5 tbsp. + 1 tsp. = ⅓ C.
8 tbsp. = ½ C. = 4 fl. oz.
1 gill = ½ C.
10 tbsp. + 2 tsp. = ⅔ C.
12 tbsp. = ¾ C.
16 tbsp. = 1 C.
1 C. = ½ pt. = 8 fl. oz.
2 C. = 1 pt. = 16 fl. oz.
4 C. = 1 qt. = 32 fl. oz.
4 qt. = 1 gal.
8 qt. = 1 peck
4 pecks = 1 bu.

Butter, margarine, solid vegetable shortening, or lard: ¼ lb. = ½ C.

Baking chocolate: 1 square = 1 oz.

Bread crumbs, fresh: 1-lb. loaf with crust = about 11 C. 1 C. = 2¾ oz.

Graham crackers: 8 to 10 = 1 C. crumbs

Gingersnaps: 20 to 22 = 1⅓ C. crumbs

Cornflakes: about 3 C. = 1¼ C. crumbs

Other wafers and crackers: 18 to 24 (depending on size) = 1⅓ C. crumbs

Egg whites, fresh: 8 to 11 = 1 C.

Egg yolks, fresh: 12 to 14 = 1 C.

Cream, heavy: ½ pt. = 2 C. whipped

Flour, all-purpose or whole wheat: 1 lb. = 4 C. sifted

Flour, cake: 1 lb. = 4¾ to 5 C. sifted

Lemon juice: 1 medium lemon = 3 tbsp. juice

Orange juice: 1 medium orange = ⅓ C. juice

Sugar, brown: 1 lb. = 2¼ to 2⅓ C. packed

Sugar, confectioners': 1 lb. (unsifted) = 4½ C.

Sugar, granulated: 1 lb. = 2¼ to 2½ C.

Sugar, maple: 1 lb. = 1¼ C.

Almonds, shelled: 1 lb. = 3 C.

Walnuts, shelled: 1 lb. = 4 C.

Pecans, shelled: 1 lb. = 4 C.

Peanuts, shelled: 1 lb. = 2¾ C.

Popcorn: 1 lb. = 2 C.

Apricots, dried: 1 lb. = 3⅔ C.

Currants: 1 lb. = 2⅜ C.

Dates: 1 lb. = 2 C.

Raisins: 1 lb. = 2 C. packed

Cranberries: 1 lb. = 4 C.

Spinach: 3 lb. = 1 peck

Coconut, shredded: 1 lb. = 6 C.

Marshmallow: 1 lb. = 4 C.

Almond paste: 1 lb. = 2 C. packed
Rice: 1 lb. = 2 C.
Tapioca: 1 lb. = 3 C.

CAPACITY OF CANNED FOOD CONTAINERS

No. 1 can = 1⅓ C.
No. 1 (tall) = 2 C.
No. 2 can = 2⅓ C.
No. 2½ can = 3½ C.
No. 3 can = 4 C.
No. 5 can = 7 C.
No. 10 can = 13 C.

HOW TO CARE FOR A NEW PLANK

Rub it well, top and sides, with salad oil. Heat on rack in very low oven (275°F.) for 1 hour. Cool. Wipe off excess oil. Plank is now seasoned and ready to use. After using, wash quickly in hot soapy water (do not soak). Rinse, dry well. Plastic food wrap, aluminum foil, or clean paper bag makes a good storage cover. Keep planks in a cool dry place.

RENDERING LARD

A penny saved is a penny earned.

> 6 qt. fat, cut in small pieces, or fat called "leaf lard"
>   from your butcher
> 1 pt. water
> 1 tbsp. salt

Put all ingredients in kettle (8 quart). Simmer slowly, stirring frequently, for 1¼ hours. Strain through cheesecloth. Put into earthenware jar and cover. Refrigerate. *Makes 2 cups.*

SEASONING SALT MIX

For your condiment shelf.

> ¾ tsp. rosemary
> ¾ tsp. sage
> ¾ tsp. dill weed
> 1½ tsp. paprika
> 1½ tsp. onion powder
> 1½ tsp. black pepper
> 1½ tsp. celery powder
> 1½ tsp. garlic powder
> 2 tbsp. MSG
> ¾ C. salt

Use all finely ground ingredients. If you can't buy them this way, use a rolling pin to rub them fine. Blend all ingredients. Keep in shaker. *Makes ½ pound.*

SPICE OF LIFE ON YOUR KITCHEN SHELF

For just enough, sniff and taste. Perfect flavor and no waste.

MEATS	VEGETABLES	SOUPS	SAUCES	SALADS	DESSERTS
Allspice	Cassia	Cassia	Cassia	Paprika	Cinnamon
Cassia	Cinnamon	Cinnamon	Cinnamon	Mace	Cloves
Cloves	Nutmeg	Cloves	Cloves		Nutmeg
Ginger	Paprika	Nutmeg	Nutmeg		Vanilla
Nutmeg	Red Pepper	Paprika	Red Pepper		
Paprika	Mace	Mace	Saffron		
Turmeric	Ginger		Turmeric		
Red Pepper			Mace		
Mace			Ginger		

PICKLING SPICES	PASTRY	POULTRY	FISH	STEWS
Allspice	Allspice	Turmeric	Turmeric	Paprika
Cassia	Cassia	Paprika	Saffron	Mace
Cinnamon	Cinnamon	Saffron	Paprika	
Cloves	Ginger	Ginger	Mace	
Turmeric	Nutmeg		Ginger	
Ginger	Saffron			
Cayenne	Turmeric			
	Mace			

KNOW YOUR APPLES

Variety	All Purpose	Pie	Sauce	Salad	Eating Raw	Baking	Months Available	Flavor
Wealthy	X	X					Aug.–Oct.	Tart–Spicy
Jonathan	X			X	X		Sept.–Jan.	Spicy–Juicy
Delicious				X	X		Sept.–April	Rich–Sweet
Grimes Golden	X		X	X	X		Sept.–Dec.	Bland–Sweet
McIntosh		X	X	X	X		Oct.–Feb.	Mild–Sweet
Cortland	X					X	Oct.–Jan.	Mild–Spicy
Golden Delicious	X	X	X	X		X	Oct.–April	Rich
R. I. Greening	X	X	X		X	X	Oct.–Feb.	Aromatic–Crisp
Stayman	X	X	X	X			Oct.–Feb.	Rich–Winy
York		X	X			X	Oct.–Feb.	Tart–Firm
Baldwin	X					X	Nov.–April	Mild–Firm
Rome Beauty			X			X	Nov.–April	Bland–Firm
Northern Spy	X					X	Dec.–Mar.	Tender–Spicy
Newton Pippin	X		X	X	X	X	Nov.–May	Tart–Crisp
Winesap		X		X	X		Dec.–May	Spicy–Sweet

DRESS UP WITH HERBS

I recall the pungent spicy odors of Mother's herb days, and the gray and green and amber leaves spread on fresh "butcher paper" on the big kitchen table, overflowing to the sideboard and wide, sunny windowsills. When the leaves were crisp and crackling, she would crush them in her palms and then store them in the spice commode that hung near the range. Each of the 24 tiny drawers had an herb label burned into the wood, and Mother would paste a dated label inside to ensure that the herb's age had not exceeded its potency.

Drying herbs is a humble task; most of us would rather pay for these seasonings than take the time to prepare them. But it is such a waste to throw away herbs that glamorize a dish as clothes do a woman. They can perk up appetizers and soups, egg and cheese dishes, meat, fish, poultry, salads, sauces, and vegetables.

The next time you cut off onion or celery tops, just wash them well and drain them. Place them in the oven to dry slowly. The same can be said of parsley, sage, mint, chives, and all other herbs. You'll adore using them, and if in doubt where they "dress up" the best, refer to my herb chart. You will be amazed to find that they all hold a unique place in the art of cookery. Remember that the secret of success in using fresh or dried herbs is subtlety. Even more mysterious and enchanting will be your efforts if you dry and use the foliage of your own herb garden.

HERB CHART

Herbs in food are as essential as cosmetics in a boudoir. Both create magic.

SOUPS	SALADS	FISH and SHELLFISH	VEGETABLES	STEWS	MEATS and POULTRY
Caraway	Anise	Angelica	Lovage	Bay	Bay
Anise	Bay	Fennel	Parsley	Parsley	Lovage
Parsley	Borage	Parsley	Caraway	Savory	Caraway
Savory	Burnet	Tarragon	Dill	Lovage	Marjoram
Tarragon	Ca away	Dill	Mint	Sage	Parsley
Bay	Chives	Garlic	Onion	Anise	Savory
Chives	Cicely	Hyssop	Rosemary	Borage	Dill
Dill	Dill	Lovage	Thyme	Celery	Garlic
Fennel	Garlic	Mint	Borage	Thyme	Hyssop
Garlic	Parsley	Onion	Garlic	Marjoram	Mint
Hyssop	Fennel	Oregano	Fennel	Rosemary	Onion
Celery	Horseradish	Rosemary	Sesame		Oregano
Balm	Hyssop	Sage	Poppy		Rosemary
Thyme	Lovage	Savory	Mustard		Sage
Marjoram	Mint	Thyme	Anise		Tarragon
Chervil	Oregano	Basil	Celery		Thyme

Rosemary	Savory	Bay	Coriander	Balm
Mint	Tarragon	Chervil	Cumin	Chives
Lovage	Thyme	Celery		Coriander
Sage	Balm	Mustard		Anise
Oregano	Onion			Cardamom
Coriander	Chervil			Mustard
Sesame	Marjoram			Celery
Cardamom	Coriander			Cumin
Cumin	Sesame			Fennel
Mustard	Poppy			
	Cardamom			
	Mustard			
	Celery			

EGGS AND CHEESE	CASSEROLES	SAUCES	STUFFING	CAKES AND COOKIES	BREADS AND ROLLS
Parsley	Thyme	Dill	Chervil	Anise	Anise
Savory	Parsley	Marjoram	Parsley	Caraway	Caraway
Chives	Bay	Parsley	Rosemary	Coriander	Lovage
Dill	Chives	Bay	Sage	Sesame	Cardamom
Onion	Marjoram	Chives	Bay	Fennel	Celery
Rosemary		Garlic	Thyme	Cumin	Coriander
Tarragon		Lovage	Balm	Poppy	Cumin
Thyme		Mint	Celery	Cardamom	Poppy
Basil		Onion	Savory		Sesame
Marjoram		Sage	Tarragon		
Chervil		Savory	Shallots		
Fennel		Tarragon	Chervil		
Caraway		Thyme			
Celery		Celery			
Coriander		Chervil			
Cumin		Rosemary			
Sesame					
Mustard					

GARNISHES:
Parsley for all vegetables
Chervil for all soups
Peppermint for fruit
Whole cloves with ham
Mustard seed on soup or fish
Sesame seed on soup

Sesame as a casserole topping
Mustard seed on eggs
Mustard on cheese
Poppy seed on soups
Sesame seed on potatoes

Index

A

Amber Marmalade, 106
Angel Meringue, 256
Angel White Frosting, 256
Anthony K's Chili Sauce, 121
Apple Brown Betty, 288
Apple Cake, 232
Apple Pan Dressing, 81
Apple "Sass" Butter, 107
Au Gratin Potatoes, 26
Aunt Dilly's Date and Nut Bread, 169
Autumn Peach Pie, 272

B

Backyard Clothespin Rolls, 187
Baked Black Walnut Frosting, 256
Baked Ham Glaze, 56
Baked Sweet Apples, 98
Baking Soda Bread, 169
Banana Fluff Frosting, 257
Brown Butter Icing, 257
Banana Nut Loaf, 170
Banana Salad, 148
Barbecued Back Ribs, 37
Basic Sweet Dough, 188
Beef Balls, 37
Beef Loaf, 38
Beef Stroganoff, 39
Berry Red Jam, 107
Black Bread, 189
Black-eyed Susan Bread, 190
Black Magic, 137
Blueberry Hill Muffins, 171
Blue Grape Conserve, 108
Bohemian Braided Sweet Bread, 191
Boiled Pour Custard, 302
Bon Bon Cookies, 208
Bordelaise Sauce, 56
Bread and Butter Pickles, 124
Breading Mix, 304
Bread Pudding, 289
Breads, 168-187
Breads, Yeast, 187-206
Breakfast Bread, 191
Brown Sauce, 56

Brown Stock, 4
Burgundy Cubed Steaks, 39
Burnt Oatmeal Soup, 7
Butter-Chocolate Filling, 258
Buttermilk Griddle Cakes, 171
Butterscotch Fruit-Nut Bars, 208

C

Cabbage, Carrot, and Raisin Salad, 148
Cabbage Salad Dressing, 160
Cakes, 231-254
Candied Chunk Pickles, 124
Candied Fruit Bread, 172
Candied Orange Peel, 91
Candied Sweet Bread, 193
Candy Gumdrops, 209
Canning and Pickling, 97-147
Caramel Cookie Tarts, 210
Caramel Dips, 258
Carrot Curlicues, 26
Carrot Marmalade, 109
Celia Tuttle's Rich Christmas Hard Sauce, 302
Cheddar Cheese Soup, 8
Cheese Sauce, 57
Chewy Fudge Brownies, 211
Chewy Oatmeal Cookies, 213
Chicken Broth, 9
Chicken Cacciatore, 72
Chicken Curry Soup, 9
Chicken Gourmet, 73
Chicken Marinade, 57
Chicken Velvet Soup, 10
Chili Con Carne, 40
Chilled Avocado Soup, 10
Chilled Cucumber Soup, 11
Chocolate Bavarian Pie, 273
Chocolate Cream Cheese Fluff, 259
Chocolate Fudge Banana Pie, 273
Chocolate Fudge Cake, 232
Chocolate Icing, 259
Chocolate Nut Chip Cookies, 211
Chocolate Supreme Icing, 259
Chocolate Yolk Frosting, 260
Chowder, 7-24
Christmas Cookie Frosting, 260

321

Cinnamon Dribble Glaze, 261
Cinnamon Mix, 261
Cinnamony Raisin Toast, 172
City Apple Pie, 274
Clarifying Stocks, 6
Cocktail Sauce for Seafood, 57
Cocktail Spread, 92
Cocoa Meringue Torte, 233
Cocoa Whipped Cream, 261
Coffee Cake Muffins, 173
Cold Beauty Preserves, 99
Company Spinach Molds, 27
Company Veal Loaf, 41
Cooked Prune Salad, 149
Cookies, 207-230
Cookie's Crackled Gingersnaps, 212
Cooking Wild Rice, 80
Corn Relish, 131
Cornstarch Pudding, 289
Cornstarch Sponge Cake, 234
Country Beet Relish, 132
Country Fried Mush, 174
Country House Stew, 41
Country Inn Barbecue Dressing, 58
Country Pot Roast, 43
Crabmeat and Shrimp Salad, 149
Cranberry Date Chutney, 132
Cranberry Salad, 150
Cranberry Sauce Salad, 150
Cream of Carrot Soup, 12
Cream of Leek Soup, 12
Cream of Lettuce Soup, 13
Cream of Parsley Soup, 14
Cream of Pecan Soup, 14
Cream of Tartar Biscuits, 174
Cream of Tomato and Mushroom Soup, 15
Cream Puff Dough, 290
Creamy French Salad Dressing, 160
Crêpes for Soup, 175
Crêpes Souzette Sauce, 300
Crêpes, Waffles, or Pancakes, 175
Crock Pickles, 125
Crunchy Butter Drops, 212
Crystallized Rose Buds, 143
Crystal Orange Peel, 100
Cucumber Mold Salad, 150
Cup Custard, 291
Currant-Spice Rolls, 194
Curry Salad Dressing, 161
Cut-Out Cookie Dough, 214

D

Dad's Green Peppers, 44
Dandelion Blossom Wine, 138
Danish Chicken Soup, 14
Danish Twist, 195
Date Bars, 214
Deluxe Egg Nog, 139
Desserts, 288-299
Dietrich's Salad, 162
Dilly Beans, 116
Dilly Rolls, 195
Double Decker Pecan Fudge, 234
Down East Oyster Stew, 16
Dressing, Salad, 160-167
Dress Up With Herbs, 313
Drinks, 137-143
Drop Dumplings, 176
"Duchess" Jam, 110
Duchess Potatoes, 28
Dutch Cheese, 144

E

Easy Barbecue Sauce, 58
Eggs Benedict, 74
Egg Salad Sandwich, 74
Eggs and Poultry, 72-78
Easy "Cuke" Relish, 132
Egg Yolk Bread, 196
Egg Yolk Sponge Cake, 235

F

Fail-Proof Hollandaise, 59
Farmer's Bread Soup, 16
Farmer's Daughter Salad Dressing, 162
Farmer's Daughter Thousand Island Salad Dressing, 163
Farm Fried Potatoes, 28
Filling, 255-270
Flambéed Bananas, 291
Flat Bread, 177
Fluffy Cheese Cake, 236
Fluffy Frosting, 262

Fluffy Meringue, 263
Fluffy Pink Salad Dressing, 163
4 Season Pickled Fruits, 101
French Fried Onion Rings, 28
French Fried Toast, 177
French Fried Sandwiches, 92
French Market Onion Soup, 17
French Soufflé Omelet, 75
Fresh Bread Crumb Dressing, 81
Fresh Peach Jubilee, 292
Fresh Strawberry Sponge Cake, 237
Fresh Strawberry Sponge Pie, 274
Frosting, 255-270
Frozen Pumpkin Pie, 275
Fruitcake Glaze, 263
Fruit, Canning, 98-105
Fruit Sauce and Variations, 301

G

Garden Chow Chow, 134
Garden Pea Soup, 17
Garlic Dressing Number One, 163
Garlic Dressing Number Two, 164
German Cole Slaw, 151
Giblet Gravy, 70
Gingerbread Man, 215
Ginger Gem Cupcakes, 238
Gingery Bread, 238
Glaze, 264
Glazes, 255-270
Glazes for Bread, 264
Gold Cake, 239
Golden Chicken Gravy, 70
Goldenrod Sauce, 60
Gold Toast, 178
Gooseberry Ketchup, 122
Graham Cracker Crust, 286
Grandma's Oatmeal Bread, 197
Grape Chiffon Pie, 275
Grape Jelly from Bottled Juice, 111
Grandma's "Crocked" Jam, 110
Grated Orange Chiffon, 240
Gravy, 54-71
Green Bean Salad, 152

Greengage Plum Jam, 112
Green Garlic Olives, 139
Green Gooseberry Pie, 276
Green Mountain Mold Salad, 152
Guide to Measuring Equivalents, 307

H

Half Moon Crescents, 216
Hamburger Potato Pie, 45
Ham Loaf, 44
Ham Stock, 5
Hard Crusted Bread, 198
Harvest Wine, 140
Haymaker's Beer, 140
Head Cheese, 145
Herb Chart, 314-317
Holiday Bread, 198
Holiday Cranberry Salad, 153
Homemade Mayonnaise, 164
Horseradish Sauce, 60
How to Care For a New Plank, 309

I

Ice Box Potato Rolls, 199
Irish Whiskey Pie, 277
Italian Meat Balls, 46
Italian Spaghetti Sauce, 60

J

Julia's Sauerkraut, 29
Jams and Jellies, 106-115
Johnny Cake, 178
J.K.'s Sourdough Rolls, 200
Julia's Raised Dumplings, 200
Jackie's Swirl Cookies, 216
Jam Drop Cookies, 217
Jumbo Sugar Cookies, 218
Jiffy Frosting, 265

K

Kandy's Medley, 153
Knightsbridge Ginger Cookies, 218
Know Your Apples, 312

L

Lancaster Red Bean Soup, 18
Lazy Cuke Relish, 136
Lemonade Pie, 278
Lemon Bread, 179
Lemon Nectar Pie, 277
Lemon Rind Pound Cake, 240
Lime Chiffon Gelatin, 292
Lobster Thermidor, 86
Luci's Anise Cookies, 219

M

Macaroni, Tuna, and Pea Salad, 154
Macaroon Angel Cakelets, 241
Maine Coast Clam Chowder, 18
Mango Chutney, 101
Manhattan Cherry, 141
Maple Crunch Chiffon Cake, 242
Maple Frosting, 265
Marinated Bean Salad, 154
Marinated Fillets, 87
Marsala Braised Pheasant, 76
Martha's Boiled Spice Cake, 242
Meat Balls in Blankets, 46
Meats, 36-52
Meringue Shells, 286, 287
Merry Christmas Cookies, 219
Merry Macaroons, 220
Mild Tomato Sauce, 61
Mixed Bean Salad, 155
Mock Caramel Filling or Topping, 265
Mock Mincemeat, 117
Mock Whipping Cream Icing, 266
Molasses-Chocolate Rolled Cookies, 221
Molasses-Oatmeal Bread, 201

Mom's Butter Bread, 202
Mom's Stuffing for Fowl, 82
Mona's Pickled Eggs, 126
Mulligatawny Soup, 19
My Mom's Roll Jam Cake, 243

N

New England Clam Chowder, 20
New England Cranberry Sauce, 62
Nut Filling, 266

O

Old Fashion Brown Bread, 180
Old Fashion Cabbage, 56
Old-Fashioned Baking Powder Biscuits, 180
Old-Fashioned Boiled Salad, 165
Old-Fashioned Bread Stuffing, 82
Old-Fashioned Rice Pudding, 293
Old Settler Lemon Raisin Pie, 279
Old Tyme Kidney Bean, 156
Old Tyme Waffle Batter, 181
Open Face Sandwich, 93
Orange Bavarian Pie, 279
Orange Candied Sweet Potatoes, 30
Orange Cranberry Relish, 102
Orange Glaze, 62
Orange Run Sauce, 63
Oxtail Stew, 47
Oyster Dressing, 83

P

Paella Barcelonesa, 88
Pan Gravy, 71
Paper-Shell Pecan Pie, 280
Pastry Creme, 266
Peach and Cherry Conserve, 112
Peach Cobbler, 294
Peanut Butter Banana Cookies, 222

Peanut Butter Oatmeal Cookies, 223
Pear Amber Jelly, 113
Pecan Coconut Frosting, 267
Penny Mission Cookies, 223
Perfect Pie Crust, 285
Persimmon Pudding, 294
Petticoat Cookies, 224
Pickled Cabbage, 119
Pickled Dried Apricots, 103
Pickled Nasturtium Seeds, 146
Pickled Pears, 103
Pickled Pepper Hash, 136
Pickled String Beans, 120
Pickles, 123-131
Pie Glazes, 268
Pieplant Conserve, 113
Pies, 271-287
Pilgrim Pumpkin Pie, 280
Pineapple Cream Salad Dressing, 166
Pineapple Upside Down Cake, 244
Pink Meringue Kisses, 221
Plain Popovers, 182
Pocket Cookies, 224
Pointers for Fruit Cake, 244
Popcorn Snowballs, 93
Popovers, 182
Poppy Seed Cake, 245
Poppy Seed Form Cake, 246
Poppy Seed Pound Cake, 247
Potato Biscuits, 183
Potato Flat Cakes, 30
Potato Pancakes, 31
Potato Puffs, 31
Preparing Converted Rice, 304
Pretty Pickled Crab Apples, 104
Prune and Nut Cake, 247
Prune, Apple, and Celery Dressing, 83
Prune Duff, 295
Prune Sauce, 301
Prune Whip, 296

Q

Quiche at the Farmer's Daughter, 75
Quick Breads and Pancakes, 168-187

R

Raisin Rocks, 225
Raisin Sauce, 64
Raspberry Vinegar, 142
Red Raspberry Chiffon Pie, 281
Red Snapper, 89
Relish, 131-136
Rendering Lard, 310
Rice Stuffing, 84
Rich White Sauce, 68
Ripe Cucumber Curls, 127
Roast Potatoes, 32
Roast Squab, 77
Royal Icing, 268
Rolled Oat Drop Cookies, 226
Rolled Oatmeal Cookies, 227
Round Steak Chunks, 48
Rump Roast, 48
Russian Salad Dressing, 166

S

Saccharine Pickles, 128
Salad Dressing, 160-167
Sand Tarts, 227
Sangría, 142
Sauce Piquante, 64
Sauces, 56-71
Sauce Tomate, 64
Sausage Apple Stuffing, 85
Scampi, 94
Sea Foam Frosting, 269
Seafood, 86-90
Seashore Salad, 156
Seasoning Salt Mix, 310
Sherry Mushroom Sauce, 65
Shiny Glaze, 269
Simple Syrup, 305
Sirloin Burger, 49
Soap, 305
Soft Brown Sugar Cookies, 228
Soup and Chowder, 7-24
Sour Cream Cheese, 282
Sour Cream Coffee Cake, 183
Sour Cream Cole Slaw, 157
Sour Cream Date Drops, 229
Sour Dough Pancakes, 184
Sour Dough Starter, 203

Southern Fried Catfish, 89
Southern Hush Puppies, 185
Spaetzels, 186
Spanish Brandy Cheese Cake, 248
Spanish Cold Vegetable Soup, 21
Spanish Peasant Bread, 203
Spice Cake, 249
Spiced Applesauce, 297
"Spice of Life" on Your Kitchen Shelf, 311
Spread for Sandwiches or Hot Hors d'Oeuvres, 95
Stained-Glass-Window Mold, 297
Steak Marinade, 65
Steamed Plum Pudding, 298
Stewed Tomatoes with Celery, 32
Stocks, 4-6
Story Book Pickles, 129
Strawberry-Banana Gelatin, 283
Strawberry-Banana Icing, 270
Strawberry-Rhubarb Pie, 283
Stroganoff Hamburgers, 50
Stuffing, 79-85
Sugar and Spice Rolls, 204
Sugared Pecans, 95
Sugar Rose Garnish, 146
Summer Shrimp Dip, 96
Sun-Cooked Peach Preserves, 105
Supreme Sauce, 66
Swedish Meat Balls, 50
Sweet-Sour Cabbage, 33
Sweet Sour Sauce, 66
Swiss Fondue Bourguignonne, 51

T

Tangerine Soup, 22
Taragon Salad Dressing, 167
Tartar sauce, 67
Teeny-Weeny Pickled Beets, 120
Ten O'Clock Pancakes, 185
Thin White Sauce (Medium and Thick), 68
Tip Top Meringue, 270
Toasted Seed Wafers, 229
Tom and Jerry, 143
Tomato-Bisque, 23
Tomato Conserve Delight, 114
Tomato Ketchup, 122
Tomato-Rice Casserole, 34
To Sauté Large Mushrooms, 33

Traditional Cinnamon Rolls, 205
Turkey and Pineapple Salad, 158

U

Up-to-Date Rice Soufflé, 299

V

Veal Balls, 52
Veal Shanks, 52
Vegetables, 24-34
Vegetable Salad, 158
Vegetables, Canning, 116-120
Veloute Sauce, 67

W

Waldorf Salad, 159
Watermelon Bowl Salad, 159
Watermelon Rind Pickles, 130
Water Rolls, 205
Wheat Gems, 186
White Angel Cake, 250
White Angel Food Cake, 251
White Bridal Cake, 251
White Pound Cake, 253
White Stock, 6
Wild Plum Jelly, 115
Wind and Water Cake, 255
Winter Corn Soup, 24

Y

Yellow Daisy Cake, 254
Yorkshire Potato Pie, 34
Yummy Drops, 230

Z

Zippy Chili Sauce, 69